As one of the
an
Thomas C

For more tha
guidebooks have unloc
of destinations aro
sharing with travelle
experience and a passion for travel.

**Rely on Thomas Cook as your
travelling companion on your next trip
and benefit from our unique heritage.**

Thomas Cook **traveller** guides

BULGARIA
Lindsay & Pete Bennett

Your travelling companion since 1873

Written by Lindsay and Pete Bennett, updated by Debbie Stowe
Original photography by Pete Bennett

Published by Thomas Cook Publishing
A division of Thomas Cook Tour Operations Limited
Company registration no. 3772199 England
The Thomas Cook Business Park, 9 Coningsby Road,
Peterborough PE3 8SB, United Kingdom
Email: books@thomascook.com, Tel: +44 (0) 1733 416477
www.thomascookpublishing.com

Produced by Cambridge Publishing Management Limited
Burr Elm Court, Main Street, Caldecote CB23 7NU
www.cambridgepm.co.uk

ISBN: 978-1-84848-389-7

© 2005, 2007, 2009 Thomas Cook Publishing
This fourth edition © 2011
Text © Thomas Cook Publishing
Maps © Thomas Cook Publishing/PCGraphics (UK) Limited

Series Editor: Karen Beaulah
Production/DTP: Steven Collins

Printed and bound in Spain by GraphyCems

Cover photography © Getty Images/Dorling Kindersley

Contents

Introduction

Once one of the mysterious countries on the other side of the Iron Curtain, Bulgaria is now fast establishing itself as a great-value mainstream tourist destination. Though relatively compact, it contains a wealth of varied attractions.

Bulgaria's main appeal is its diverse geography, with beaches, mountains, forests and historic villages all within fairly short hops. Warm Balkan hospitality – aided not least by some excellent wines and a hearty cuisine – a healthy dose of culture and still low eastern European prices help seal the deal. A trip to Bulgaria has a little something for everyone, whatever your age, whatever your predilection.

Nature has bestowed bountiful gifts, the most important of which for the modern holidaymaker are superb beaches and warm summer days. Tourists from all across Europe, and from Russia, too, flock to the grand strands of the Black Sea coast for simple relaxation and a first-class suntan. In the winter months the appeal of hot sand gives way to the allure of soft snow as skiers and snowboarders head for the mountain slopes. Bulgaria is the number one destination for good-value skiing packages and its snow record is second to none in Europe.

Bulgaria caters admirably to its 'snow bunnies' and 'beach bums', but there's so much more to discover about this intriguing place. The countryside invites exploration. Outside the main holiday hotspots, tourists are still few and far between and it is replete with treasures – natural and man-made. UNESCO has recognised nine sites as important enough to be placed on the World Heritage list. That's an impressive number for such a small nation.

The country's long and complicated history has bequeathed architecture galore, from ancient Neolithic and Thracian times to the present day. Bulgaria is rich in religious art, displayed in over 100 incredible Orthodox monasteries, many of which are still living religious communities, but these vie with the 19th-century National Revival architecture as the country's pièce de résistance. This physical embodiment of a newborn spirit that flourished in the wake of independence from Ottoman power is uniquely Bulgarian and can be seen at its best in several 'living museums', where a thriving contemporary populace breathes life into the protected stones and wood.

Bulgaria is a land of wide-open spaces, panoramic vistas and natural abundance. Farming still moves with the rhythm of the seasons and often at a pace of one horse-power (with real hooves) rather than the many of the internal combustion engine. The tools of yesteryear can still be seen here; scythes for reaping and wooden pitchforks for turning the hay. Everything operates on a more human scale.

Mountains are a salient feature of the landscape and they entice you to discover their hidden passes and sparkling lakes along numerous forested trails. The country has several eminent national parks and nature reserves protecting rare ecosystems. Birdlife abounds all year round, and there are still small populations of wolves and bears.

Still in a transition phase following decades of communist rule, Bulgaria has set its sights westward and joined the EU in 2007. Though the pace of change is often too slow for the EU's liking, things are beginning to become westernised. Visit now and you'll get to experience the blooming of a fresh, new and captivating destination, and you'll beat the rush that is starting to follow.

A still-unspoilt landscape is one of Bulgaria's main attractions

The land

Bulgaria sits in the heart of what's historically been called the Balkan region – officially defined as that part of southeast Europe bounded by the River Danube to the north, the Ionian and Adriatic Seas in the west, the Aegean and Black Seas in the east and the Mediterranean to the south.

The Balkan Mountains (called the Stara Planina in Bulgaria itself) comprise several separately named ranges and run through Bulgaria from the Serbian border to the Black Sea.

The limits of the modern state are defined by the Danube to the north (the border with Romania); the Black Sea to the east; and land borders with Turkey and Greece to the south and Serbia and Macedonia to the west. Sofia sits close to modern Bulgaria's western boundary.

Though the Balkans hit the headlines in the 1990s due to extensive bloody internecine strife (with the regions of Bosnia, Serbia and Kosovo being the most prominent), Bulgaria remained untouched by, and detached from, the violence.

Regions

This book divides the country into six sections. The capital obviously merits a chapter, followed by a short section on excursions from Sofia, to entice those only visiting the city to explore the beautiful countryside that's just on the doorstep.

The Black Sea coast is a deserved stand-alone section, while the rest of the country is divided into three chapters – Central Bulgaria (the central valley along with the Stara Planina and Sredna Gora Mountains), the Southwest (covering the Pirin, Rila and Rodopi Mountains) and the North (roughly corresponding to the southern plain of the River Danube).

Climate

The climate of Bulgaria is complicated. The north is dominated by continental air masses from the Russian steppes while the south sits at the northern limit of the Mediterranean sphere. This clash of systems can cause stormy weather and extremes of temperature in summer or winter. However, there are numerous regional variations, especially in the more remote valleys.

Winters tend to be long, with heavy snows in the mountains from

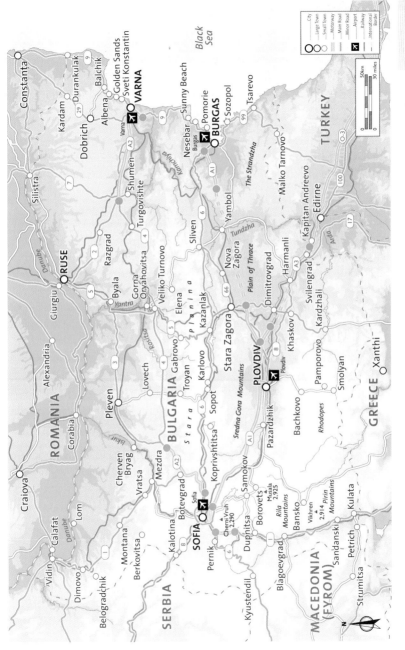

December to May, but temperatures are slightly milder on the Black Sea coast, which sees more rain. Summers are long and hot, with an average temperature of 24°C (75°F), but higher in the west around the capital and lower in the Black Sea area, where the heat is tempered by offshore breezes.

Rain can be expected at all times of year but is a particular feature of the spring and autumn.

Topography

For a relatively small country, almost 111,000sq km (43,000sq miles), Bulgaria's topography is extremely varied.

Almost 30 per cent of the country's land mass is mountains, with more than 30 peaks over 2,000m (6,500ft). These, and their corresponding valleys, have played a major part in the moulding of Bulgarian lifestyle and Bulgarian character – a self-reliant population of insular mountain folk and arable farmers in the leas and meadows of the lowlands. The Stara Planina mountains divide the country and shape the weather. They halt the southerly track of the harsh winter steppe winds and interrupt the northerly progress of very dry heat from the Mediterranean in summer, affecting the native flora and fauna and the development of agriculture throughout the country.

Each mountain range has its own distinct appeal. The alpine peaks of the Pirin are in marked contrast to the karst (eroded limestone producing sinkholes, fissures and ridges) of the Blue Rocks and the Ropotamo basin or the gently rounded knolls of the Sredna Gora. Bulgaria is equally rich in underground landscapes. Some 4,300 caves and caverns constitute a veritable hidden world that's played an important role in Bulgarian history – protecting its population, its religion and its national heritage.

Farming is often still done the traditional way throughout Bulgaria

Water also plays an important role. The snows and rain of the mountains divert into numerous drinkable springs and streams – the country has rarely been short of water, as the verdant landscape suggests. Though the country has no major rivers aside from the Danube on its northern frontier, it has a plethora of splendid lakes, many making for 'chocolate box' landscapes.

Bulgaria's only coastline is that in the far east of the country, on the Black Sea. Here you'll find splendid and renowned sandy swathes (the jewels of Bulgaria's tourism industry), rocky peninsulas, marshes, reed beds, sand dunes, and fresh and saltwater lakes.

The hot summers are ideal for sunflower crops

Flora and fauna

Bulgaria has some of the most widely diverse flora and fauna in Europe; hundreds of rare species survive in the many untouched landscapes and in the dozen or so national parks.

The country supports several thousand species of plant. Over 30 per cent of the land mass is forest, of which the majority is virgin, the best being in the UNESCO-protected Pirin National Park and the numerous species of trees in the Strandjha National Reserve.

Three-quarters of all European bird species can be found here, of which many are classed as rare. Environments such as the Black Sea coast and the numerous lakes offer ideal environments for native and migratory waders and water species, while the mountains and pastureland offer a refuge to songbirds and birds of prey.

Animal species include bears (*see p137*), wolves, wild goats and deer. The rivers and the Black Sea provide habitats for 200 species of fish, a small number of otters and seals, and, even more rare, the bottlenose dolphin. Entomologists will also find Bulgaria a fascinating destination, with over 27,000 species. (Mosquitoes could be the main ones you encounter if you don't take precautions throughout the summer and on humid spring and autumn nights.)

Bulgaria stands to benefit greatly from environmental tourism if the process is well managed; however, environmental groups are concerned that the rapid development of a post-communist Bulgaria will put pressure on these valuable natural riches. Hunting, logging, fishing and pollution are also a cause for anxiety.

History

Sitting at a crossroads of east and west, Bulgaria has witnessed waves of invasions, some peaceful but many bloody and unwelcome. This constant movement of peoples and change in rule overlays a fervent desire for national self-determination that has seen short-lived but long-remembered times of Bulgarian home rule. The most recent development has been the country's emergence from the grip of Soviet influence.

Peoples

Bulgaria's first recorded inhabitants were the Thracians, an ancient tribe who peopled what is now northern Greece and southern Bulgaria. They were a sophisticated people whose art and culture influenced the Greeks, who in turn founded settlements in what is now Bulgaria, and the Romans, who conquered the whole of the Balkans. When the Roman Empire split, the Eastern or Byzantine section, with its capital at Constantinople (present-day Istanbul), grew in power to be the pre-eminent Empire at the end of the 1st millennium AD. The church spread its Orthodox Christian message across Eastern Europe, a legacy that is strong to the present day in Bulgaria. This influenced the style of religious architecture and religious art until the arrival of the Ottomans. The Byzantines fought with the Slavonic and Bulgar peoples for control of Bulgarian lands from the 5th century to 1185.

The majority (an estimated 85 per cent) of today's Bulgarian population are said to be descended from the Slavs, a peaceful farming people, who arrived in the region from the Carpathian Mountains in the north. The Bulgars arrived in the region from the east; a warlike people, they subjugated the Slavs and remaining Thracians and Greeks, but gradually the disparate groups grew together into a Bulgarian nationality, helped by the founding of the first Bulgarian Empire in the 7th century. The Turkish Ottoman Empire conquered and ruled Bulgaria from 1396 until 1878; around 9 per cent of the present population are Turks, direct descendants of the Ottomans. They were persecuted after the Ottoman defeat but since the fall of communism have organised themselves politically and now hold an important minority power base on today's political scene. They are to be found mostly in settlements close to the Turkish border and live alongside the Pomaks in the

Rodopi Mountains. The Pomaks, said to number around 250,000 in Bulgaria, where they are known as Bulgarian Muslims, are Slavs who converted to Islam during Ottoman rule.

Bulgaria's multi-ethnic mix is completed by the Roma, or gypsies, who constitute around 4.7 per cent of the population. These people live on the margins of society and have suffered oppression since the fall of communism; however, they have begun to organise political representation.

Recent history

The Balkan Wars at the beginning of the 20th century resulted from the collapse of the Ottoman Empire. The region gained its freedom at different times and was claimed as part of the territory of one or another fledgling Balkan state, or struggled to found its own government while at the same time the greater powers of Europe (the French, British, Germans, Austro-Hungarians and Russians) sought to gain influence or meddle in the new country's affairs. Bulgaria tried to expand its territorial boundaries (particularly in Macedonia) but was opposed by its neighbours Serbia, Romania and Greece.

During World War II Bulgaria entered on the Axis side when it realised that it was powerless to stop German forces massing on its northern border in Romania, but refused to declare war on the Soviet Union. Bulgarians also resisted Nazi demands to hand over the estimated 50,000 Bulgarian Jews. A national resistance was organised within the country by communists (and others) opposed to the fascist interim government set up after the death of the king.

In 1944 Russia declared war on Bulgaria and invaded. In September 1944, the fascist government was replaced by a new interim government, 'The Fatherland Front' – a coalition that included the communists. In November 1945, the coalition won the first free elections but it was destabilised by the communists, who gained a majority in the National Assembly. A new Soviet-style constitution was declared in September 1946. This lasted until November 1989.

The royal family was forced to go into exile in 1946, but Simeon Sakskoburggotski, the man who would have been king, returned in 2001 and formed a party that ruled until 2005. In August 2005, the Bulgarian Socialist Party won the elections and Sergey Stanishev took over as prime minister.

In 2009 the Citizens for European Development of Bulgaria party gained power and Boyko Borisov became prime minister. The next presidential elections are due during 2011.

Bulgaria joined NATO in 2004 and the European Union in 2007. However, this did not herald entirely plain sailing. In 2008, the country had EU funds worth hundreds of millions of euros suspended because it failed to tackle corruption and organised crime, an accusation levelled again in 2010.

History timeline

***c.* 6000** BC   Neolithic peoples inhabit the caves of the Rodopi Mountains.

***c.* 5000** BC   The Thracian peoples settle areas of what is now Bulgaria and northern Greece. They were influential on the art and architecture of the Greeks and Romans who followed.

***c.* 700** BC   Greek seafarers settle on the Black Sea coast.

345 BC   The Macedonian people from what is now northern Greece invade Thracian territory.

***c.* 80** BC   The Romans invade southern Bulgaria, establishing a regional capital at Varna.

AD **46**   The Roman occupation of the Balkans is complete. Ulpia Serdica (Sofia) is now the capital of Thracia (Bulgaria).

National Revival Pantheon, Ruse

c. 200	As the Roman Empire begins to collapse, Bulgaria is threatened by northern tribes (Vandals, Huns and Goths).
330	The Roman world is divided, with Eastern Europe falling under the auspices of the Byzantines at Constantinople (now Istanbul).
c. 475	Slavs from the Carpathian Mountains settle in the region to farm.
c. 550	Warlike Bulgars arrive from the east.
681	The First Bulgarian Empire is proclaimed by Khan (or Tsar) Asparukh.
681–1018	Slavs, Bulgars and Thracians develop a peaceful understanding as the Empire expands. Tension with the Christian Byzantines is constant and fighting breaks out sporadically.
c. 860	Tsar Boris I converts Bulgarians to Christianity.
893–927	The Empire is at its height under Tsar Simeon, with a capital at Veliki Preslav, but Simeon's attempt to capture the Byzantine throne backfires.
1018	The first Bulgarian Empire comes to an end as the people are assimilated into the Byzantine Empire.
1185	An uprising leads to the Second Bulgarian Empire (including parts of modern Serbia and Hungary) with a powerful capital at Veliko Turnovo.
1396	Ottoman Turks invade Bulgaria, bringing to an end the Second Empire.
1400s–1800s	Ottoman rule. Christianity is persecuted but religious fervour is kept alive in the remote monasteries. Some Slavs convert to Islam, becoming 'Pomaks'.
1762	Monk Paisii Hilendarski completes the first comprehensive history of the Slav-Bulgarian people, kick-starting the Bulgarian National Revival.
1870	The Ottoman Turks recognise the Bulgarian Orthodox Church.

Monument in Vratsa to freedom fighter and national hero Hristo Botev

1876	April Uprising against Ottoman rule is brutally put down.
1877	Russia declares war on the Ottoman Empire in defence of the Bulgarian people. Estimates put the death toll at 200,000.
1878	Treaty of San Stefano ends the Russo-Turkish War with vast tracts of the Balkan peninsula now independent Bulgarian soil.
1878	The Treaty of Berlin rewrites the map as Western Europe fears too much Russian influence in the region. A smaller Bulgaria becomes an independent state but this treaty creates artificial boundaries that still haunt the Balkans today.
1879	The Bulgarian constitution is adopted.
1885	Border problems cause short-lived war with Serbia. Western Europe then recognises an expanded Bulgaria.
1912	First Balkan War against the Ottomans. Bulgaria, Serbia, Greece and Montenegro conquer Macedonia and parts of Thrace.
1913	Second Balkan War, against Serbia, Romania and Greece, breaks out over sovereignty of other lands released by the Ottomans.
1915	Bulgaria enters World War I on the German side.
1939	Bulgaria declares its neutrality at the start of World War II.

1941	Bulgarian authorities allow German troops to enter the country. They declare war on Britain and France but not on Soviet Russia.
1943	King Boris III dies in mysterious circumstances soon after a tense meeting with Hitler.
1946	The People's Republic of Bulgaria is proclaimed with a constitution based on Soviet Russia's communist system. The country is led by Georgi Dimitrov, Vasil Kolarov for less than a year, and then, from 1950, by Vulko Chervenkov.
1962–89	Todor Zhivkov takes control and Bulgaria becomes one of the most successful economies in the Eastern Bloc.
1985–9	Perestroika weakens the foundations of the communist system across Eastern Europe.
1989	An internal coup within the Communist Party brings an end to Zhivkov's rule. The Communist Party opens up the Bulgarian political arena and changes its name to the Bulgarian Socialist Party. A group of other parties comes together under the banner Union of Democratic Forces (UDF).
1990	The Bulgarian Socialist Party sweeps to victory in the first national elections since the fall of communism.
1990–97	Seven ineffectual governments in seven years cause the collapse of the Bulgarian economy. Bribery, organised crime and corruption are rife.
2001	The exiled former Bulgarian King Simeon II forms a political party, the National Movement. Simeon wins the June elections, becoming prime minister, while ex-communist Parnavov becomes president.
2004	Bulgaria becomes a member of NATO, breaking irrevocably with its Eastern Bloc past.
2007	Bulgaria becomes a member of the European Union (EU).
2013	Bulgaria's target date for joining the Eurozone.

Orthodoxy and the monasteries

An Orthodox monk

the words of the Gospel to the Slav people in their own language rather than in Latin. This involved translating the Bible into Slavic, a tongue for which there was no written language. The brothers set about devising an alphabet (originally called Glagolitic) incorporating all the sounds of Slav. By the year 900 this had developed into the standard Cyrillic script still in use today.

The development of the written language took place during the era of Bulgaria's First Empire. Its capital Veliki Preslav was the most powerful in the Balkans. The fact that the Bulgarians could worship in their own language was immensely important. The seeds of a new Bulgarian national identity planted by Boris and successive Bulgarian tsars thrived through use of this new language, and were nurtured by Bulgarian Orthodoxy.

The founding of religious communities became a fashionable practice; Bulgaria's leading religious community, Rila, was established at this time around the charismatic hermit/monk Ivan Rilski. The royal family and upper echelons of the court made major bequests to the

Monasteries have played a pivotal role in the development of Bulgarian society and culture in the centuries since Tsar Boris converted the population to Christianity c. AD 860.

In the early 860s, two brothers Kiril (Cyril) and Metodii (Methodius) (*see box*) were invited by the pope to carry

Dryanovo Monastery

most influential religious orders. The huge influxes of cash, precious gifts and relics allowed monasteries to employ the finest masons, woodcarvers and artists for the building and decoration of their complexes, giving rise to a golden age of religious art and handicrafts.

In their turn, the monasteries repaid this patronage with their steadfastness throughout the years of Ottoman rule. They protected the faith and became the repository of Bulgarian culture in the written word, and traditional religious art in the face of a religion that was implacably opposed to iconic images as a basis for worship. Furthermore, as the yoke of Ottoman power grew heavier over time, they provided help on a practical level, offering succour and

sanctuary to the freedom fighters who sought to rid the country of foreign influence.

Orthodoxy rose like a phoenix from the ashes in the wake of the Ottoman withdrawal from the Balkans in the late 19th century. Today it is emerging from behind the shadow of communism into a 21st-century Bulgaria driven by a market economy. It remains to be seen whether the monasteries will survive as thriving religious communities or simply end up as the country's primary tourist attractions.

CYRIL AND METHODIUS

Brothers Cyril (*c.* 827–69) and Methodius (*c.* 815–95, some say 826–85) were born in Thessalonika (now in Greece) where their father was serving in the Byzantine army.

They didn't enter the priesthood immediately. Methodius followed his father into the military before becoming a monk, while Cyril (christened Constantine) chose teaching and philosophy, being at one time the chief archivist at the library in Byzantium.

The brothers travelled together throughout the Balkans, evangelising. After Cyril's untimely death, Methodius became papal delegate to the Slavic region.

In the following centuries many universities and libraries in the Balkans were named after the brothers, who were pronounced 'protectors of Europe' by Pope John Paul II.

The website *www.bulgarianmonastery.com* offers more information on each of the monasteries featured in the **Destination guide** (blue) section as well as less significant monasteries out of the scope of this guide.

Politics

After the fall of communism in the late 1980s, Bulgaria changed, in 1991, to become a parliamentary representative democratic republic, with a multi-party system and a National Assembly. The president is directly elected and has a five-year term of office, with the right to only one re-election.

Post-communist Bulgaria

Bulgaria didn't make a brilliant start. There were eight governments between 1989 and 1997, none with a grasp of the complexity of the job in hand. The change to a market economy caused economic meltdown, not helped by rampant corruption and the proliferation of a Bulgarian 'mafia' – a phalanx of ex-secret service officers and party officials – who were making good profits on protection rackets and money laundering.

In 1999 a new left-wing coalition with reasonably firm foundations set about introducing a series of programmes under the collective banner 'Bulgaria 2000' – designed to prepare the country for the new millennium. The plans included the revision and decentralisation of many government functions based on EU-approved models.

Then in 2001 came the surprising, almost fairy-tale development that held the promise of a sustained new beginning. Ex-King Simeon declared that he was returning to the country permanently and furthermore he was going to found a political party and run for elected office.

Though public demand for a constitutional monarchy was weak (only 15 per cent of those questioned

EX-KING SIMEON

Born in Sofia in 1937, the young Prince Simeon of Saxe-Coburg-Gotha inherited his title at the age of six following the untimely and mysterious death of his father Boris III in 1943.

Immediately after World War II the family returned to Bulgaria, but in a referendum the population rejected the constitutional monarchy and Spain offered the young king asylum.

Simeon received his education in Alexandria, Madrid and military college in the United States, following which he became a successful businessman and worked tirelessly on behalf of Bulgarian exiles with many national and international bodies. After the fall of communism he first visited Bulgaria in 1996, a full 50 years after his discomfiting departure.

THE BULGARIAN FLAG

The post-communist Bulgarian flag is composed of three horizontal bands – white, green and red. White represents the land, green represents the natural riches of the countryside and red represents the courage and resilience of the people.

felt it appropriate), the ex-monarch was still a very popular figure. Founded only two months before the elections, the new National Movement Simeon II Party took first place and Simeon was inaugurated as the new prime minister, the first European monarch ever to have gained civil power following the loss of the throne. He remained prime minister until 2005.

By 2002 the Bulgarian economy was slowly and painfully turning the corner. The monetary unit, the lev, was linked to the euro and inflation was stable at a moderate 3.8 per cent. The country began to look outward from its domestic crises and forge a coherent foreign policy. It ameliorated the crisis in Kosovo by allowing ground support forces of the UN to land and coordinate their peacekeeping strategy, and it finally broke completely with the old Soviet Bloc by joining NATO in March 2004.

Its sights were now firmly set on closer ties with Europe and the country joined the EU in 2007. Bulgaria's EU-inspired reforms and the gradual process of integrating more with the West brought increasing prosperity, and its economy expanded at a rapid rate up until 2008. Like many other countries in the region, Bulgaria was hit hard by the global financial crisis and went into recession. Nonetheless, the changes brought about by EU membership look to have irreversibly put the country on a new path towards ever greater westernisation.

The constitution

The Bulgarian constitution upholds the National Assembly as the sole legislative body. It comprises 240 members elected every four years by proportional representation. The National Assembly then elects the prime minister.

The president is the head of state. Elected every five years, the president can serve a maximum of two terms in office.

A council of 12 judges ultimately protects the constitution and the rights of citizens. They are subject to elections every nine years.

Parliament Building, Sofia

Culture

Bulgaria's culture is inextricably linked with its battle for national self-determination. The nation's self-image has been forged from its long and titanic struggles against the Byzantines during the First Bulgarian Empire, the Ottomans during the Second Bulgarian Empire and communism during the latter part of the 20th century.

The Bulgarian National Revival period in the late 19th century (*see pp26–7*) was the joyous expression of a people free from a heavy yoke. In present-day Bulgaria it is difficult to overestimate its importance in representing all that is good in the arts.

The role of the Church

Perhaps more than in any other country in the world, the Church features as an important national presence, working for cultural, not just physical and spiritual, survival. In addition to nurturing Bulgarian arts and crafts, the Bulgarian Orthodox Church also acted as the custodian for important, rare and sometimes illegally produced books, allowing a newly liberated Bulgaria to re-engage with its history and heritage in the wake of the Ottoman withdrawal.

The freedom fighters

The fight for freedom from the Ottoman Empire was never a peasant-led movement. The revolutionary committees comprised intellectuals, poets, writers and scholars, and they galvanised the common people with their call to arms. Chief among these was the poet Ivan Vazov (1850–1921). His works included titles such as *Deliverance, Epic of the Forgotten* and the novel *Under the Yoke* (1893), describing life in a Bulgarian village under Ottoman rule that epitomised the struggle of the whole population. Poet Hristo Danov (depicted on today's 50 leva banknote) became one of the first post-independence publishers, helping to bring Cyrillic texts to the general population. Georgi Danchev, a classicist, is the most renowned artist of the period between independence and World War II.

The growth of the arts in the post-Ottoman period

Several opera houses and theatres were built in the late 19th and early 20th centuries to cater to rising demand for performances. The National Academy of Arts was also formed in 1896 to formalise the burgeoning genres. However, most artistic development took place within the metaphysical boundaries of the national experience of Ottoman oppression. Expression in literature and music often focused attention inwards to Bulgarian tradition rather than exploring influences from the greater world.

Dobri Hristov (1875–1941) is considered the father of modern Bulgarian classical music. Born in Varna, he collaborated closely with Antonín Dvořák. Hristov inextricably linked Bulgarian classical music with the lilt, structure and cadence of traditional folk tunes. Another luminary, Emanuil Manolov (1860–1902), composed the first Bulgarian opera, *Siromahkinia*. However, Pancho Vladigerov embraced a more mainstream Western tradition and is better known outside Bulgaria.

In the literary world, Greek-born Atanas Dalchev (1904–78) wrote well-received poetry during the 1920s and 1930s and poet/writer Elisaveta Bagryana (1893–1991) also published her best works at this time.

Painting was evolving too – moving from the classic to more experimental styles, taking into account the arrival of Impressionism and Surrealism in Europe. Anton Mitov, son of a master icon painter, was at the forefront of the movement, along with Jaroslav Věšín.

The impressive St Dimitar Church in Veliko Tarnovo

Ruse Theatre

The arts under communism

Even before the end of World War II, the steely reach of the Soviet regime cast a dark shadow over the arts. Rayko Alexiev (1893–1944), a renowned cartoonist and writer, was beaten to death by unknown culprits after publishing several anti-Soviet cartoons. This set the scene for communist rule. All forms of 'western-style' composition in words and music were classed as subversive. Artists had to toe the line or fall from favour, or worse.

However, folk music was considered close to the socialist ideal and was encouraged, which strengthened the Balkan classical genre, cadences of folk music introduced by Dobri Hristov (*see previous page*). Lubomir Pipkov was a successful proponent of the approved 'socialist realism' musical style, and Philip Kutev, famed for his ability to adapt folk music for the grander stage, received particular acclaim. Only later in the era, during the 1970s and 80s, did young composers such as Tsenko Minkin and Stefan Dragostinov begin to push the boundaries, experimenting with new musical forms.

During communist rule, members of the Writers' Union were paid for each work they produced, as long as it fitted the strict pro-Soviet criteria, no matter what the sales. This, and having to work within the constraints of the system, stunted creativity. Criticism in any form, even through the arts, was punished. Poet Blaga Dimitrova (1922–2003) was at first fêted by the communist authorities then vilified and dropped from the inner circle, and Antanas Dalchev chose to remain creatively silent throughout the Zhivkov era.

The best-known Bulgarians went into exile rather than work under the Soviet yoke. The most famous of these is perhaps Georgi Markov (1929–78). The dissident writer was working as a broadcaster for the BBC World Service in London when he was struck with an umbrella tip while waiting at a bus stop. The tip deposited a small pellet containing a lethal dose of the poison ricin into his leg. He died three days later.

Others include artist Christo (Javacheff), born in 1935 in Gabrovo, renowned for his 'packaging' art – large-scale projects including the packaging of 11 islands in Biscayne Bay in Miami with pink polypropylene walls – and Stephen Groueff (1922–2006), a Bulgarian political immigrant who was most famed for his book *Crown of Thorns*.

Still, the communist regime's patronage of the arts was generous. Funding of companies and training for the gifted was as important as their better-known sports programmes, which produced a generation of sporting superstars. Opera was a particular success, with Nickolai Guaurov and soprano Raina Kabaivanska making their presence felt in a competitive genre, as well as Boris Christoff (1914–93), considered one of the greatest basses in opera history.

The arts in post-communist Bulgaria

Since the fall of communism, intellectuals and artists have suffered a considerable downturn in fortune. State funding is almost non-existent and when the economy plunged into freefall in the 1990s it left the population no money for the 'higher' pursuits. There was an exodus from Bulgaria and many artists left for Europe and the United States, including critic Alexander Kiossev and writer Ivaylo Ditchev.

Young composers such as Angel Stankov and Jossif Radionov have won domestic and international acclaim for their work. The most successful writer in Bulgaria during the early 1990s was Hristo Kalchev (1968–2006), with his title *The Wrestlers* – an exposé of the

ACROSS THE GALAXY

A traditional Bulgarian folklore tune, *Izlel e Delio Haidutin*, from the Rodopi region, was one of the songs chosen to be included in a CD representative of 'Earth music' that was part of the cargo on the Voyager spacecraft launched in the 1970s to communicate with any other life forms in our solar system. The songs were chosen to express as fully as possible traditional musical forms from across the planet.

Bulgarian mafia – while writers Zlatomir Zlatanov and Rumen Leonidov, novelists Deyan Enev and Alek Popov, and poet Kristin Dimitrova all carry the torch forward into the third millennium.

The major enduring problem for writers and poets continues to be reaching a wider market and having the opportunity to be published in a language other than Bulgarian. It's also a problem that continues to hinder an outsider's enjoyment of the work of these influential thinkers.

Varna Opera House

Festivals and events

The range of festivals and events in Bulgaria is wide, reflecting the diverse lifestyles of the country. World-acclaimed celebrations of performing arts sit side by side with age-old festivities – including traditional costumes, local dances and reverential religious processions. Every crop has its own 'harvest festival', from the grape to the grain.

The following is a list of the major festivals and events that take place each year around the country, but for further details on arts festivals *see p153*.

January
St Basil's Day, or **Survaki**. Children visit neighbours to wish them Happy New Year with a bunch of twigs, and villagers don animal masks to parade (1st)
Yordanovden, or **St Jordan's Day**, when Christ's baptism in the River Jordan is marked by men jumping into rivers to retrieve a cross (6th)

February
Trifon Zarezan, wine-producing areas. Vines are sprinkled with wine for good luck (1st or 14th)

March
Baba Marta, or **Granny March**. Spring-cleaning takes place in rural homes to symbolically see out winter. People also exchange red and white threads, or *martenitsa*, for good luck (1st)

Kukeri, Shiroka Lûka (first weekend)
Music Days Festival, Ruse (last two weeks of the month)
Sandanski Celebrations (Thursday after Orthodox Easter)
International Film Festival, Sofia *www.cinema.bg/sff*
Annunciation Day (25th)

May
Balkan Folk Festival, Veliko Turnovo (10 days in the early part of the month)
International Plovdiv Spring Fair (one week mid-month)
Festival of Classical Music & Ballet, Sofia. Main venue is the National Palace of Culture, *www.ndk.bg*

SUPER-FEST!

The largest of Bulgaria's festivals is the internationally recognised Koprivshtitsa Folk Festival; however, it is only held every five years (next in 2015). The website *www.carnaval.com/bulgaria* will keep you up to date with folklore festivals in Bulgaria and the greater Balkan region.

Gergyovden, or **St George's Day**. Sheep are sacrificed and roasted to mark the end of spring

Festival of Bansko Traditions (one week mid-month)

Varna Summer Festival – the highlight of the summer along the Black Sea coast, lasting from May to October, *www.varnasummerfest.org*

June

Fire Dancing Festival, Bulgari, Strandjha Nature Park (early in the month)

Festival of the Roses, Kazanluk and Karlovo (early in the month)

International Festival of Chamber Music, Plovdiv (10 days mid-month)

International Folklore Festival, Veliko Turnovo (three weeks late June–mid-July)

July

Burgas and the Sea Song Contest (two months through July–August)

Sofia International Folklore Festival (late in the month)

August

Feast of the Virgin Mary, nationwide celebrations (15th)

International Folklore Festival, Plovdiv (early in the month)

International Jazz Festival, Bansko (around the second week), *http://bansko-jazz.com*

Folklore Festival, Koprivshtitsa (mid-month, every five years)

Oreshak Annual Fair (mid-month)

Pirin Sings, Bansko (held mid-month in even-numbered years)

Love is Folly International Film Festival, Varna (one week either late August or early September)

International Folklore Festival, Burgas (late in the month)

September

Rozhen Fair (8th, every four years)

Apollonia Arts Festival, Sozopol. Live concerts (first two weeks of the month, *www.apollonia.bg*)

International Plovdiv Fair (one week late in the month)

Night of Museums and Galleries, Plovdiv (last weekend)

December

Skiing season (starts around the middle of the month)

Festivals keep the country's song and dance traditions alive

Bulgarian National Revival

Traditional door detail

The Bulgarians had lived under Ottoman domination for over 300 years. Their religion, customs, lifestyle and language had all been suppressed. The essence of Bulgarian religious orthodoxy and culture survived in remote monasteries, kept alive by a small number of monks; the heart of Bulgar/Slav identity seemed to have been lost in the mists of time. However, in the mid-1700s a monk named Paisii Hilendarski set about compiling the first history of the Balkan region – putting into words the heroic feats of Asparukh, the first Bulgarian Tsar, Boris, who unified the people under Christianity, and Simeon, who ruled during a period before the first millennium when the Empire was at its zenith. The tome was completed in 1762 but even then, had it rested on some dusty library shelf, it might have become simply another academic thesis. However, Hilendarski set out on the 18th-century equivalent of a promotional tour and his book caught the public imagination.

The seeds of a renewed identity began to take root just as the shackles of Ottoman rule began to weaken. Orthodoxy emerged from the shadows, the Bulgarian language began to be taught in newly opened schools and a generation of Bulgarians took over the mantle of trade and industry from a declining Turkish mercantile class. This new breed of entrepreneur used its wealth to build fine new houses and patronise the arts for the first time in several generations. Bulgarian craftsmen were suddenly in high demand for traditional building and woodcarving, and every large Bulgarian town had a gentrified district built in a style known as Bulgarian National Revival. Along with

A typical National Revival window

Among the best places to see National Revival architecture are:

Etur, an artisan village re-created using original 19th-century buildings (*see p58*).

Koprivshtitsa, home of the Bulgarian royal family during Ottoman rule (*see pp60–62*).

Melnik, surrounded by the best vineyards in Bulgaria (*see pp84–5*).

Shiroka Luka, in the heart of the Rodopi Mountains (*see pp94–5*).

Plovdiv (alongside architecture from other eras – *see pp87–90 & 96–7*).

Tryavna, famed for its woodcarvers (*see pp67–9*).

Veliko Turnovo, capital during the Second Bulgarian Empire, reinstated in the late 19th century (*see pp70–75*).

this renewed national confidence came a renaissance of the arts (*see pp20–21*). Homes, public buildings and churches reflected the new aesthetic and artistic ideal.

There are no set architectural rules for National Revival style – unlike, say, the Georgian neoclassical style of the 1700s in the UK – but the emphasis is on beauty as part of the daily lives of citizens. Large stone mansions stand in voluminous verdant walled gardens. The exteriors of the buildings have brightly painted façades, latticework wooden soffits, awnings and balconies. Interior decoration is characterised by intricately carved wooden ceilings, wardrobes and chests and brightly patterned rugs, carpets and cushions.

Renovated building, Koprivshtitsa

Impressions

Bulgaria is a multidimensional destination. The Black Sea is an obvious attraction for beach lovers and families, while the mountains offer endless outdoor pursuits and fantastic landscapes. Although the capital, Sofia, would never claim to have the historical sights of Prague, it is a likeable and friendly city with some fascinating museums and galleries.

For general sightseeing, Bulgaria is a compact country and there's something remarkable in every region, whether it be an impressive monastery, a historic village, mineral springs or traditional artisans. You could easily combine some or all of these in a two-week holiday, or spend longer and savour your favourites.

When to go

Bulgaria calls itself a year-round destination, and it is true that it provides activities throughout the year, but be aware that many attractions and activities are highly seasonal. The Black Sea season lasts from May to October, with an ultra-busy period from late June to the end of August. In the winter

Sofia's skyline in winter, with Mount Vitosha towering behind

The Pirin Mountains in summer

the coastal resorts are deserted and almost all hotels are closed.

The skiing season runs from December to April, though there's often enough snow left in May to enjoy a few runs, especially in Bansko (which has the best snow record). Most package tours to the ski resorts stop just after Easter, so you'll need to travel independently to ski after that date.

Hiking can commence in the mountains almost as soon as the snows have melted, and stops as the snows arrive. It can be hot for walking in July and August, but spring and autumn are ideal seasons. The same is true for general touring or visits to the capital.

Most of Bulgaria enjoys a covering of snow in the winter, and because it sits at the boundary between two massive weather systems it can be prone to extremes of every condition. Impressive thunderstorms can happen at all times of year and rain is also a possibility whatever the season.

How to get around

Bulgaria has limited domestic air services because the distances are not great, the infrastructure is too expensive and the demand isn't there. The only viable route is the Sofia/Black Sea service and you can travel all year round to Varna and Burgas, with more services running May–October only.

Trains are a good way to get to the main cities and towns. It's possible to tour from Sofia to Plovdiv, Veliko Turnovo, Ruse, Varna and Burgas on trains of reasonable quality, but it does mean that many of the country's most interesting sites (certainly the monasteries and most of the mountains) will be out of reach.

Really the only way to see the best of what Bulgaria has to offer is to take to the roads. This is a bit of a problem, since the roads are generally in poor

The Black Sea is a pleasant destination, especially between May and October

condition, but those willing to drive (with care) will reap major rewards, because then small villages and quiet mountain footpaths will be brought within your reach.

If you don't want to drive, chartering a car with driver, or a taxi, for the day is an affordable option. This way someone else is taking the strain of driving but you still control the itinerary and time. This could easily be combined with train travel, so that you use major towns as a base to explore by charter vehicle. Alternatively, take a coach tour to the various attractions. The disadvantage of this is that you hand over control of the visit to your tour guide.

What to wear

Layering is the byword here. Summer temperatures reach above 30°C (86°F), so light cotton or breathable clothing is advised, but even in August if you intend to head to the hills it's wise to carry a warm layer (a fleece is ideal). Spring and autumn could still be warm, so keep the light cotton outfits, but a couple of warmer layers, especially for the fresher evenings, and even one cold weather option should be part of your wardrobe. In the winter months, warm and waterproof clothing is a must throughout the country but especially in the mountains.

If you are going to be doing a lot of hiking then specialist boots are

advised. Ski equipment can be rented in the resort but you'll need your own ski-suit (or separate jacket and trousers) for the slopes.

Monasteries

The Bulgarian monasteries are not as strict as their Greek counterparts in enforcing a dress code. Shorts and vests seem not to be a problem. However, it is still wise to wear, or carry with you, items of clothing that will cover the thighs and shoulders. Remember these are supposed to be spiritual places where the demure dress of the monks should be a pointer to your own clothing.

Cultural aspects
Red tape

Bulgaria's entry into the European Union in 2007 removed – or at least reduced – much of the bureaucracy that visiting this former communist state used to entail. Some sources still advise foreigners to register with the police, though it is unlikely that not doing so will present any problems. Should you be handed any official-looking piece of documentation, it's still probably worth hanging on to it – just in case.

Cyrillic

In addition to the usual foreign words encountered in a new overseas holiday destination, you've got a whole new alphabet to get to grips with! Thank St Cyril for that (*see p16*). However, in Sofia and on the Black Sea you'll see numerous helpful signs showing the Roman equivalent spellings on road signs and English menus in restaurants, and, with Bulgaria's entry into the EU, more and more roads are being signposted in both the Cyrillic and Roman scripts for towns and villages.

Most people working in the tourist industry will speak some English, but it's a little more challenging in the countryside where, at present, you'll need to brush up on your body language to navigate successfully.

You'll find that maps, road signs and guidebooks don't have standard Roman

Many signs are now in Roman and Cyrillic script

Quality hotels, like this one in Pomerie, come at very reasonable prices

spellings for many towns – this is because it's difficult to translate the sounds of some Cyrillic letters directly into English – particularly ъ. This letter is pronounced as a short 'u' in English but is often spelt as 'a' or 'â' on maps – e.g. Veliko Târnovo as opposed to Veliko Turnovo.

For more details about spelling and pronunciation see the Language section (*pp184–5*).

Prices

Bulgaria is a cheap destination to visit, and the tendency, once common, in hotels and some restaurants to charge foreigners a different (higher) rate, is decreasing all the time. Bulgarians earn

well below the average Western salary and, while the lot of the average Bulgarian has improved, some still perceive foreigners to be wealthy.

The best way to get a good deal on hotel rooms is to pre-book through a travel agent. Rack rates can be reduced considerably but it obviously means you've got to plan your whole itinerary in advance.

Food is still very good value, even though, when there is a menu in Cyrillic as well as one in English, you might pay more. In the Black Sea resorts restaurant prices can be 50 per cent higher than inland, but since few Bulgarians can afford to stay there this isn't dual pricing, it's just the market rate.

Yes or no?

Bulgarians shake their head for yes and nod for no (although the nod is a mostly upward movement). This can cause a lot of confusion in terms both of their answers to your questions and of your reaction to their queries. Think about your natural reaction to the question, 'Would you like milk with your coffee?' A short nod for yes will result in a black coffee arriving!

STREET NAMES

The following abbreviations have been used throughout the book:

bul. – bulevard, meaning avenue/boulevard.

pl. – ploshtad, square.

ul. – ulitsa, street.

To confuse the issue further, many Bulgarians who work or have worked with foreigners will use a nod for yes and shake their head for no because they know this is the norm for us.

To keep communications clear it's probably better to say *da* (yes) and *ne* (no) rather than use non-verbal communication.

Remember
There's a lovely tradition throughout the country of posting obituaries outside the houses of the recently bereaved and also in public areas such as town halls and post offices. Although it's not possible to understand the sentiment

Religious icons are all around, such as this one in Veliko Turnovo

FLORAL *FAUX PAS*

If invited to a Bulgarian home, always take a small gift. Flowers are popular but make sure you take an odd number of blooms. Even-numbered bouquets are for funerals only.

expressed in Cyrillic, the pictures of the people are fascinating and poignant.

Smoking
Bulgaria is a smoker's country. A ban on lighting up in public places was first revoked then watered down. Non-smoking sections are becoming more common though – in general, the more upmarket the place, the more likely it is to have one. During the summer it is less of an issue, as people can eat and drink alfresco.

Birthdays and saints' days
Most Bulgarians are named after an Orthodox saint and people celebrate their annual saint's day with even more gusto than their actual birthday, because Petars, Kirils or Sophias across the country can get together to party.

Tourist information
Official tourist information is poor, with few tourist offices. For background information, try these websites:
www.mfa.government.bg
English-language section of the official government website, with information on visas and formalities.
www.travel-bulgaria.com
General travel information on Bulgaria.

Impressions

Sofia

Set majestically in the lee of the Vitosha Mountains on an elevated plateau, Sofia is one of the highest capitals in Europe. A city of a million and a quarter people, it reflects the turbulent antecedents of the country but also the challenges facing a Bulgaria on the brink of a new era. Here a few horse-drawn carts still vie for road space with brand-new BMWs and Mercedes, and at Orthodox churches teenagers in the latest skimpy Western fashions beseech the saints in the flickering light of a votive candle.

Sofia was founded at a point equidistant between the Black Sea and the Adriatic and thrived as an important staging post on trade routes travelled since antiquity. The earliest settlement on this site was Thracian Serdica. It went through a number of name changes, including Roman Ulpia Serdica and Byzantine Triaditsa, before taking the name Sofia, probably from the St Sofia Church (*see p41*), during the Second Bulgarian Empire (1185–1396). Under Ottoman rule it was a regional administrative headquarters, and then was chosen as capital of the independent country in 1879.

Today the downtown area is compact and eminently walkable. Several wide boulevards radiate out from the central ploshtad Sveta Nedelya, flanked by elegant public buildings such as the National Assembly and Law Courts. Sofia is a city of statues and monuments and it's hard to find a square or road

intersection without a plinth, obelisk or statue. Many relate to Bulgaria's gratitude for Russia's help in ousting the Turks from their soil, though native heroes are not forgotten – from Vasil Levski to St Cyril.

Arkheologicheski Muzey (Archaeological Museum)

Housed under the domes of the Buyuk Djami (Great Mosque) built in the last decade of the 15th century, the Archaeological Museum is the oldest museum in Bulgaria and opened in 1879. The surprisingly small collection is organised in chronological order and there are good examples of ancient mosaics and Roman statuary, as well as Thracian finds brought from sites across Bulgaria. The coin collection is one of the finest in the world, with over 150,000 items.

ul. Saborna. Tel: (02) 988 2406; www.naim.bg. Open: May–Oct daily 10am–6pm; Nov–Apr Tue–Sat 10am–5pm. Admission charge.

Central Sofia (*see walk pp44–5*)

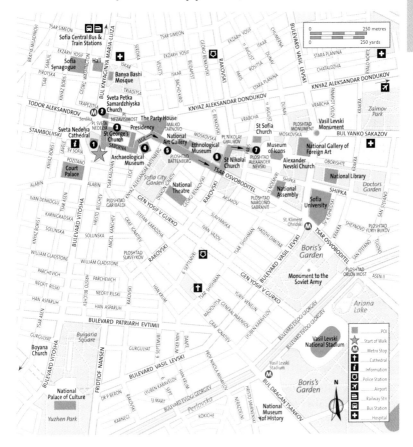

Boyanska Tsurkva (Boyana Church)

Listed as a World Heritage Site by UNESCO, tiny Boyana Church houses what are arguably the finest murals in the Balkans. The church, set in the foothills of the Vitosha range in a southwestern suburb of the city, was completed around 1250 and has almost 100 paintings.

The majesty of the murals is immediately apparent. Rich in their depth of colour and with a remarkable lifelike quality in the faces not seen in European art until the Renaissance 100 years later, the panels in the nave show the Bulgarian royal family in their fine robes. Other scenes depict stories from the Bible and there is an exquisite face of Christ in the apse cupola.

Boyana Church, whose paintings influenced religious art throughout the region

Work to preserve the original murals is ongoing and visitors are only allowed to spend 10 minutes inside the chapel, so in order to allow more time to study the detail a **Museum of Boyana** has been built next to the church. This displays copies of many of the finest murals and shows a short film in English about the church.

ul. Boyansko Ezero, Boyana. Church: tel: (02) 959 0939; www.boyanachurch.org. Open: Apr–Oct daily 9.30am–6pm; Nov–Mar daily 9am–5.30pm. Admission charge; combined ticket with National Museum of History available. Guided tours in English (separate charge). Museum open same hours, separate admission charge. Bus 64 or minibus 21.

Dzhamiyata Bashi Banya (Banya Bashi Mosque)

The last serving mosque in the city, Banya Bashi was built in the mid-16th century at the height of Ottoman power by the Turkish architect Sinan, the founding father of classical Islamic architecture. It is still used for worship and its singular lack of iconic images offers an interesting contrast to the Orthodox churches in the city.

bul. Maria-Luiza. Open: daily 8am–9pm except during prayer sessions, especially on Fridays. Women should be modestly dressed. Free admission.

Etnografski Muzey (Ethnological Museum)

Occupying one wing of the imposing former Royal Palace (1893) built in

Palladian style but with an Art Nouveau interior, the Ethnological Museum has an exceptional range of Bulgarian arts and crafts dating from around the 1700s to the present day. The galleries here are the perfect place to acquaint yourself with the fine craftsmanship in embroidery, woodcarving and ceramics before you venture out to buy souvenirs for yourself. Particularly beautiful are the national costumes still worn in so many parts of Bulgaria during folk celebrations. The museum displays illustrate the background to traditional ways of life throughout the country and its major religious festivals.
pl. Battenberg. Tel: (02) 987 4191. Open: Tue–Sun 10am–6pm. Admission charge.

Gradskata Gradina (Sofia City Garden)

Right in the heart of town, tiny Sofia City Garden is where locals like to take time out during the day to read a book, eat lunch or simply relax; you'll usually find groups of retired men playing chess, and there are one or two cafés where you can take coffee.
Between bul. Tsar Osvoboditel and bul. General Gurko at ul. Battenberg. Open: 24 hours.

Katedralata Sveta Nedelya (Sveta Nedelya Cathedral)

The symbol of Sofia, sitting at the very heart of the city, the cathedral was completed in 1863 on foundations from the Middle Ages but completely destroyed in a bomb blast in 1925 (an unsuccessful attempt on the life of King Boris III, who was worshipping there, though it killed 120 other worshippers). The church was rebuilt in neo-Romanesque style with an exceptionally ornate interior, but the highlights are the icons painted by Stanislav Dospevski, a Bulgarian artist who was born in Pazardzhik.

Sveta Nedelya is one of the busiest churches in the capital, as workers call in at lunchtime or between meetings to light a candle and say a prayer. It is fascinating to see young and old, rich and poor alike keeping the Orthodox faith alive.
pl. Sveta Nedelya, at the corner of buls Vitosha and Stamboliiski. Tel: (02) 987 5748. Open: daily 7am–7pm. Free admission.

Banya Bashi Mosque

The Ethnological Museum is located in the former Royal Palace, as is the National Art Gallery

Khali (Hali)

Built in 1910 in late National Revival style, the Hali is the largest covered market in the city and the place to watch the bustle of everyday life for the citizens of Sofia.

bul. Maria-Luiza, opposite the Banya Bashi Mosque. Tel: (02) 917 6106. Email: c-hali@bulinfo.net. Open: daily 7am–10pm. Free admission.

Muzey na Ikoni (Museum of Icons)

This collection of sacred images is Bulgaria's most important and is a must for lovers of religious art.

Housed in the crypt of the Alexander Nevski Church (*see pp34–6*), the icons date from the 13th to the 19th centuries, offering a perfect opportunity to explore the subtle changes in style and interpretation in the genre over the centuries. Several major pieces have been rescued from Nesebur (*see pp108–11*) and Sozopol (*see pp112–14*) on the Black Sea, where many churches have fallen into disrepair, while others come from monasteries around Bulgaria.

pl. Alexander Nevski. Tel: (02) 981 5775. Open: Tue–Sat 10am–12.30pm & 2–6pm. Admission charge. Guided tours in English are available.

Natsionalna Galeria za Chuzhdestranno Izkustvo (National Gallery of Foreign Art)

The largest gallery in Bulgaria houses an eclectic collection of art from across the globe. It's short on 'recognised' masters, though it does have works by Rembrandt, but the strength of the collection is in its African and Asian tribal art, which has some exceptionally well-chosen pieces.

ul. 19 Fevruari, pl. Alexander Nevski. Tel: (02) 988 4922;

www.foreignartmuseum.bg. Open: Wed–Mon 11am–6.30pm. Admission charge, free last Mon of month.

Natsionalen Istoricheski Muzey (National Museum of History)

Housed in the former Zhivkov presidential palace, this museum brings together the many strands of Bulgaria's complicated past.

The galleries have permanent exhibitions starting with Thracian treasures and then moving on to Roman artefacts found principally at Varna and Veliko Turnovo. Later exhibits shed light on Ottoman rule – including religious persecution and political life – and the role of Russia in Bulgarian independence in the late 19th century. Of course the Bulgarian National Revival period is not forgotten, with exceptional arts and crafts displays. Throughout the permanent galleries you'll find captioning in English but the background detail is only in Cyrillic.

The third floor of the palace holds temporary exhibitions allowing study of different aspects of Bulgarian history in more depth, but captions are generally not in English.

Vitoshko Lale 16, Boyana. Tel: (02) 955 4280; www.historymuseum.org. Open: Apr–Oct daily 9.30am–6pm; Nov–Mar daily 9am–5.30pm. Admission charge and additional charge for use of a camera. Combined ticket with Boyana Church available. Bus 63, 111, minibus 21 or trolleybus 2.

Sofia City Garden (see p37)

Natsionalna Khudozhestvena Galeria (National Art Gallery)

Sharing the former Royal Palace with the Ethnological Museum, the National Gallery of Art houses a collection of over 12,000 pieces by 19th- and 20th-century Bulgarian masters, including many works by the Motev dynasty, who were prolific artists throughout this period. The gallery also has an active programme of temporary exhibitions.
pl. Battenberg. Tel: (02) 980 3325; www.nationalartgallerybg.org. Open: Tue–Sun 10am–6pm. Admission charge.

Partien Dom (The Party House)

Just around the corner from the Balkan Sheraton, there is no mistaking the imposing neoclassical building that comes immediately into view. This was the headquarters of Bulgaria's Communist Party, and the large red star that hung from the top was pulled down when protestors tried to set the building on fire in August 1990.
pl. Nezavisimost. Not open to the public.

Roman remains

There are tantalising glimpses of the old Sofia in a couple of locations in the city. Behind Banya Bashi Mosque is the most imposing, the walls of a 6m (20ft) brick turret from the fort of Ulpia Serdica, built in the 3rd century AD but renovated during the second Bulgarian Empire.

Several metres of wall have also been preserved in the underpass opposite the presidency, showing Roman and Byzantine levels.

Sofiyskata Sinagoga (Sofia Synagogue)

One of only a handful of synagogues in Bulgaria and the largest in the country, the Sofia Synagogue was completed in 1910. A small museum tracing the history of the Jews in Bulgaria has useful captions in English and there is an interesting visit with an English-speaking guide. The opening times appear to be flexible, so just knock at the door to see if a visit is possible.
ul. Ekzarh Yosif. Tel: (02) 983 1273; www.sofiasynagogue.com. Open: Mon–Fri 9am–4pm, Sun 10am–2pm. Admission charge.

Tsurkvata Aleksandar Nevski (Alexander Nevski Church)

Built as a memorial to the over 200,000 Russian, Bulgarian, Ukrainian, Moldavian, Finnish and Romanian troops who perished in the Russo-Turkish War of 1877–8, Alexander Nevski is the largest Russian Orthodox church in the Balkans. Named after a renowned 13th-century Russian warrior who was the patron saint of Tsar Alexander II, the church was designed by Pomerantsev, a noted Russian religious architect of his day, and decorated by the finest artists in Europe. It was begun in 1904 and completed in 1912.

The edifice is an elegant ensemble of Romanesque arched window detail, copper cupolas and gilded domes offering an ever-changing architectural line as you view the exterior. The interior is a vast open space with three naves and has capacity for 5,000 people. The 46m (150ft) high dome is supported by massive columns. Italian marble is the material mostly used for columns, floors and the patriarch's throne. The walls are decorated with now-faded murals, and the dusty shafts of light from the few windows give the church a rather sombre atmosphere.

The crypt of the church now houses the Museum of Icons (*see p38*).
pl. Alexander Nevski. Tel: (02) 988 1704. Open: daily 7am–7pm except during services. Free admission, donations welcomed.

Tsurkvata Sveta Petka Samardzhiyska (Church of St Peter of the Saddlemakers)

From ground level only the terracotta tiles of the roof of Sveta Petka Samardzhiyska Church are visible.

Sveta Nedelya Cathedral (*see p37*)

It was a Christian place of worship built during the early years of Ottoman rule, explaining its low position and rather humble exterior. You can reach the church from the pedestrian underpass that runs under Nezavisimost Square where it meets pl. Sveta Nedelya.

While the exterior of the church was designed to be as plain as possible, the interior was a riot of bright murals depicting scenes from the New Testament. Today, although they have lost much of their lustre, they form an important example of how Orthodoxy was sustained under Muslim rule.

pl. Sveta Nedelya. Open: daily 7am–6pm. Admission charge.

Tsurkvata Sveti Georgi (St George's Church)

The oldest extant building in Sofia, St George's Church was erected as a secular rotunda by the Romans in the 4th century AD. It was converted into a Christian place of worship sometime during the early Middle Ages and then into a mosque during the Ottoman era. Damaged during World War II, it was rebuilt and renovated in the late first millennium Romanesque style. The earliest wall murals in the interior date from the 10th century.

Behind the Sheraton Hotel. Open: summer daily 8am–6pm; winter officially daily 8am–5pm but can vary. Free admission, donations welcomed.

Tsurkvata Sveta Sofia (St Sofia Church)

The city's patron and namesake St Sofia is venerated at this 6th-century Byzantine church erected during the reign of the Emperor Justinian, who also supervised the building of the great St Sophia Church in Constantinople (now Istanbul). The church was the centre of Orthodox worship during the Second Bulgarian Empire but the Ottomans added minarets during the 1400s after they took control of the area. Following damage during a series of earthquakes, the church was totally rebuilt at the start of the 20th century, and curiously it kept its minarets during the rebuilding even though the Ottomans had lost power in the area. Few of the wall frescoes have survived but the church does own a lock of the hair of pre-eminent Bulgarian freedom fighter Vasil Levski (*see pp78–9*).

Alexander Nevski Church

ul. Parizh, pl. Alexander Nevski.
Open: summer daily 7am–7pm; winter
daily 7am–6pm except during services.
Free admission, donations welcomed.

Tsurkvata Sveti Nikolai
(St Nikolai Church)

Funded by Russian émigrés in the years
just before the Revolution (1912), this
archetypal Orthodox church built by
Russian artisans from the Moscow
School of Decorative Arts is one of the
landmarks of Sofia. Though the highly
coloured ornate exterior is much
photographed, the highlights lie within
the renovated interior, with frescoes
from the Novgorod School. The icon of
St Nikolai Chudotvorets is revered as
'the wonder worker' and you'll find a
steady stream of worshippers humbly
requesting his help.

The golden onion domes of St Nikolai Church

ul. Tsar Osvoboditel. Tel: (02) 986 2715.
Open: daily 7.45am–6.30pm except
during services. Free admission,
donations welcomed.

Yuzhen Park (Yuzhen Park)

Situated southwest of the town centre,
Yuhzen Park is another place where city
dwellers come to relax. It's a good place
to bring children, as there's a funfair
with rides, and it's a great place to meet
Bulgarian families, especially at
weekends and during holidays.

The park was planned around the
imposing NDK National Palace of
Culture, Bulgaria's largest arts,
entertainment and exhibition venue (*see
Entertainment, p153*) with 16 separate
halls and theatres. Designed in sombre
'socialist' style, it was opened in 1981.

Yuzhen has two memorials of
interest. The monumental 1300
Anniversary Monument, erected in
1981 to commemorate the founding
of the First Bulgarian Empire, is now
a crumbling wreck surrounded by a
high fence to stop people getting
injured. Much more evocative is the
memorial to those who died at the
hands of the communist regime.
A simple wall of marble etched with
the names of the lost stands next to a
tiny chapel.

*Corner of bul. Vitosha and bul. Patriarh
Evtimii. Open: 24 hours.*

Walk: Central Sofia

Central Sofia is very compact and you'll be able to take in many of the major sights on the route of this 2.5km (1¹/₂-mile) walk. How long it takes really depends on how long you spend admiring the churches or how interesting you find the museums, but allow 2 hours for the walk itself.

Start at the central hub of the town, pl. Sveta Nedelya, one of the busiest parts of the city for traffic and people.

See map on p35.

1 Katedralata Sveta Nedelya

The cathedral sits at the heart of the square. Completed in 1863, it had to be rebuilt in 1925 following a bomb attack.

Leave the square by taking the underpass under pl. Nezavisimost, keeping the Sheraton Hotel immediately to your right. You'll find Sveta Petka Samardzhiyska Church here, sitting incongruously in the shadow of the contemporary city.

2 Tsurkvata Petka Samardzhiyska

This Orthodox church was built during the early years of Ottoman rule in the 14th century. It had to be inconspicuous so as not to compete with the mosques of the city. The interior has some splendid murals.

Retrace your steps back to pl. Sveta Nedelya and leave by ul. Saborna (keeping the Sheraton building on your left). Take the first left into the quadrangle behind the hotel to find St George's Church.

3 Tsurkvata Sveti Georgi

This is the oldest building in Sofia, built as a rotunda by the Romans and converted into a church in the early Christian era (*see pp40–41*).

Return to ul. Saborna and continue for the short distance to its intersection with ul. Lege, where you'll see the Archaeological Museum across the street to your left.

THE BATTENBERGS

Because the Bulgarians hadn't had royal rulers since 1396, there was no strong bloodline to claim the throne. Alexander Battenberg was a German Prince (the Battenberg family originated in Hesse), elected to the Bulgarian throne with the title of prince. The Battenbergs were well connected with most royal houses in Europe, including the Russian, Greek and British royal families. Because of anti-German feeling during World War I the British branch changed their surname to the more English-sounding Mountbatten. Prince Philip, Queen Elizabeth II's consort, is the most famous Mountbatten today.

4 Arkheologicheski Muzey

This interesting collection of ancient artefacts is housed in the Great Mosque, built in the late 1400s.

From the entrance of the museum turn right into pl. Battenberg, but if it's close to the hour wait here to see the changing of the guard at the presidential offices on the far side of ul. Lege.

5 Ploshtad Battenberg

Battenberg Square is the heart of 'Third Empire' Sofia, totally redesigned when the city became capital of a newly independent Bulgaria. Sofia City Garden lies on the right after the imposing central bank building. This is a good place to stop for a coffee. On the left is the long elegant façade of the former Royal Palace, now the Ethnological Museum and the National Art Gallery.

From the museum/gallery entrance turn left, leaving the square along bul. Tsar Osvoboditel. At the intersection of ul. Rakovski 150m (160 yds) further on is St Nikolai Church.

6 Tsurkvata Sveti Nikolai

Built by Russian émigrés in 1912, its ornate interior is furnished with many earlier icons (*see pp41–2*).

From the church, turn left along ul. Rakovski. On the right 100m (110yds) further on, pl. Alexander Nevski comes into view.

7 Ploshtad Alexander Nevski

One of the finest vistas in the city, with the domes of the eponymous church framed by an avenue of trees.

Walk: Central Sofia

You can see plenty of ancient exhibits at the Archaeological Museum

Sofia environs

Sofia is blessed with a delightful selection of attractions just on the doorstep. Less then an hour by car from the capital you can find 'Bulgaria in microcosm', magnificent nature in the form of mountain landscapes, lakes and gorges; cultural and historical sites; and the opportunity to enjoy a variety of outdoor pursuits.

Priroden Park Vitosha (Vitosha National Park)

Twenty-two thousand hectares (55,000 acres) of protected mountains overlook Sofia, pressing into the suburbs of the capital. Vitosha is the capital dwellers' playground and is known by everyone as 'the lungs of the city'. They flock to the slopes for winter skiing, summer hiking, or simply to escape the urban smog – especially at weekends, when the city is empty but Vitosha is packed with Bulgarians enjoying family picnics or romantic trysts.

That said, on weekdays there are opportunities to enjoy more peace and quiet, and if you are on a short break to Sofia rather than touring the whole country, a trip to Vitosha gives you an impression of what you are missing – majestic landscapes – plus panoramic long-range views of the city in the valley below.

Strangely, although it gives its name to the park, Mount Vitosha is not the highest peak in the mountain range. That accolade goes to Mount Cherni Vruh (The Black Mount), at 2,290m (7,513ft) the fourth highest in the country. The mountain suffers from cloud cover on average 250 days a year, so don't be surprised if it's not visible during your stay. A feature of the range is the *moreni*, 'rivers of stone', which are characterised by huge granite boulders

Vitosha National Park chairlift

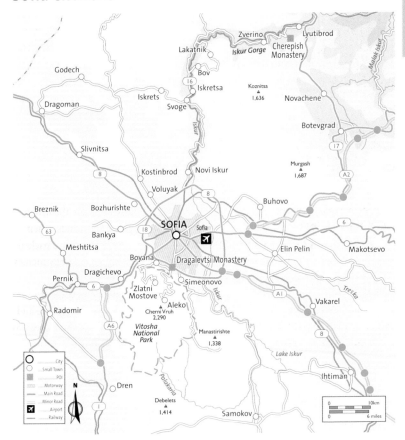

Sofia environs

filling the river valleys; they were carried down the mountain aeons ago by glaciers that melted at the end of the Ice Age and deposited them here.

The upper elevations of the park are accessible by car on its northern side, but it's much easier to take either the (two-person open) chairlift from Dragalevtsi (Драгалевци) (bus services from the Hladilnika bus station) or the gondola (six-person enclosed) from

Simeonovo (bus services also from the Hladilnika bus station), both on the lower slopes just outside the city. *Tel: (02) 989 5377; www.park-vitosha.org*

Aleko

Aleko is a popular starting point for summer hikes and climbs, and winter skiing, including the longest cross-country skiing trail in the country. From here it's a gruelling 90-minute

climb to the summit of Cherni Vruh (though you can take the chairlift to Maluk Rezen, from where it's a less strenuous 30-minute route).
Bus 66 from Hladilnika bus station accesses Aleko and there is a hotel and restaurant where the bus terminates. From here it is a 5-minute walk to the ski slopes and equipment can be hired here.

Zlatni Mostove
This small mountain settlement lies on the northern slopes of the Vitosha range. Its name means 'golden bridges', a reference to the gold panning that used to take place in the river here. Some say that it's still possible to spot the odd fleck shining in the sandy shallows, so you may be able to profit from your trip!

Zlatni Mostove is famed for its *moreni*, impressive gigantic granite glacial boulders that are now blanketed in a veneer of moss, which smother the course of the River Boyana.

A footpath links Boyana Church (*see pp35–6*) with Zlatni Mostove. Some sections are steep and the route should take about 5 hours on a round trip.
(Bus 261 from Hladilnika bus station, Sofia.)

Dragalevtsi Manastir (Dragalevtsi Monastery)
Dragalevtsi was erected in around 1350 and was once one of 14 monasteries that dotted Vitosha, collectively known as the Mala Sveta Gora ('little Mount Athos' – a reference to the holy collection of monasteries on Mount

Lake Iskur is a magnet for watersports enthusiasts

Dragalevtsi Monastery

Athos in Greece). A hotbed of dissent during the 17th century, it became a hideout for Bulgarian freedom fighters, playing host to Vasil Levski for many months. Much of the early complex was lost during battles with the Turks but the church has some interesting murals dating from the 1460s.

(Buses 64 and 93 from Hladilnika bus station, Sofia.)

Ezeroto Iskur (Lake Iskur)

The damming of the River Iskur (also spelt Iskår on many maps) has created this huge artificial lake 40km (25 miles) to the southeast of the city, which acts as a magnet for watersports enthusiasts. To find the lake simply follow the numerous vehicles sporting windsurfers or pulling trailers carrying kayaks and canoes.

A few enterprising businesses have sprung up renting equipment to tourists or Bulgarians who don't own their own, but this is an industry that has plenty of capacity for development. Many non-sporting city dwellers head to Lake Iskur for a long lunch on the sunny terrace of one of the many lakeside restaurants, where freshwater lake trout is often on the menu.

Iskursko Defile (Iskur Gorge)

Though the River Iskur circumvents the capital, the path of the river north of Sofia has some exceptional natural features. The gorge stretches 156km (97 miles), but by far the best stretch lies between Svoge and Lyutibrod, less than 40km (25 miles) from the capital. The sheer walls of granite rise over 100m (330ft) above the river valley, sheltering a series of pretty agricultural villages. The karst landscape has created several large caves, the spectacular 80m (260ft) Skaklya Waterfall, and the naturally eroded Kutinski Pyramids just north of Novi Iskur. It plays host to several monasteries, including Cherepish (*see p125*) and the Sedemte Prestola Monastery, founded in the 11th century, the church of which is unique in Bulgaria in having seven naves and iconostases (three flanking each side of the main nave).

IT'S A DATE

The birth of the Bulgarian sport of hiking began on 27 August 1895, when Bulgarian writer and philosopher Aleko Konstantinov invited the population of Sofia to join him in a mass walk from the city centre to the summit of Mount Cherni Vruh (2,290m/ 7,513ft). Over 300 people turned out for what must have seemed a rather eccentric excursion, but it started a trend that soon became the height of fashion.

Drive: Around Vitosha National Park

This eight-hour excursion allows you to leave central Sofia and enjoy some of the historical and natural attractions just on the doorstep of the city. You could combine it with a hike in Vitosha National Park, as there are many easy footpaths that don't require specialist footwear, but carry a warmer/waterproof layer.

Distance: 260km (160 miles).

Set out from Sofia down the arterial route heading southwest (bul. Makedonika becomes bul. Totleben then bul. Tsar Boris III) in the direction of Kulata. At the intersection with the Sofia ring road (bul. Nikola Petka)

turn left towards Plovdiv, then 750m (820yds) later turn right on ul. Alexander Pushkin. Behind a small maze of streets is Boyana Church (ask for directions to the Boyana Museya).

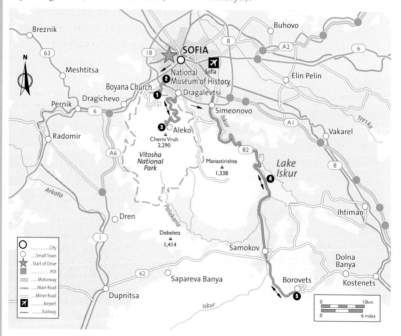

1 Boyana Church

This tiny UNESCO-listed church has some of the most remarkable medieval frescoes in the Orthodox world, but you must visit the interior, as the exterior is of rather uninspiring plain brick.

Retrace your route back to the ring road and turn left. Immediately on your right you'll find the old presidential residence set in verdant parkland.

2 Natsionalen Istoricheski Muzey (National Museum of History)

Bulgaria's premier museum is housed in a former presidential palace. Within the museum there is a vast collection of artefacts and culturally important pieces reflecting the complicated past of Bulgaria.

Continue on the ring road, still in the direction of Plovdiv. 4km (2½ miles) on from the museum you'll come to a crossroads; take a right, signposted Dragalevtsi and Aleko. The road leads through Dragalevtsi village and past the Dragalevtsi chairlift (if you don't want to drive up the hill then take this scenic open lift) and then begins to climb out of the valley up towards Aleko.

3 Aleko

As the road twists and turns you'll get exceptional views back down over Sofia on the plateau below. Finally after 7km (4¹/₂ miles) you will arrive at the end of the road (literally) and the small car park at Aleko. There is a hotel restaurant and bar here and marked (well worn) footpaths across the hills.

From Aleko go back to the ring road. Take a right again, following signs for Plovdiv. After 10km (6 miles) another crossroads offers a right turn on the A82 in the direction of Samokov. Take this turn and follow the road 27km (17 miles) to Lake Iskur.

4 Novi Iskur

This man-made lake was created when the River Iskur was barraged, and it's now a watery playground for the city dwellers. The best way to see the lake is to stop at a roadside restaurant.

From here it's only a further 30km (18½ miles) to Borovets through the town of Samokov (15km/9½ miles).

5 Borovets

Borovets is Bulgaria's premier ski resort but it's worth a visit at any time of year. In summer, you can peruse the souvenir stalls, hike in the hills, hire a horse for a cross-country trek or enjoy some refreshment at the bottom of the pistes.

Head back to Sofia and return to downtown via bul. Tsarigradsko Shose.

Enjoy spectacular mountain views

Drive: Around Vitosha National Park

Drive: The Iskur Gorge

This impressive natural gorge lies less than an hour from central Sofia. The views are dramatic but are matched by the traditional rural lifestyles in the villages along the valley floor. If you have packed your crampons and pitons, this is the place to try your hand at mountaineering – on the challenging, precipitous gorge walls.

Time: 6 hours. Distance: 125km (78 miles).

Head north out of Sofia on bul. Rozhen in the direction of Novi Iskur. You'll pass one of the city's major markets on your left when bul. Rozhen becomes route 16. You'll soon find yourself in a shallow valley where the major occupation is agriculture. Small farms and old-style methods can still be seen here with many horse-drawn carts and ploughs. You'll pick up the River Iskur 3km (1³/₄ miles) south of Novi Iskur, then you'll arrive in the town.

1 Novi Iskur

Novi Iskur is the gateway to the gorge. From here you can walk around 90 minutes west to the Kutinski Pyramids, an unusual natural rock formation caused by erosion. It's also possible to drive there in about 20 minutes.
Beyond Novi Iskur the road and river now shadow each other along the valley floor, vying for space with the railway line. A bright modern sign in Roman lettering announces your arrival in Svoge (40km/25 miles north of Sofia).

2 Svoge

This town of around 9,000 inhabitants sits at the confluence of the rivers Iskur and Iskretsa. It has a small history museum and St Paraskeva Church, with some interesting 17th-century murals.
Beyond Svoge the gorge is at its most dramatic. The river is flanked by sheer walls of grey limestone some 100m (330ft) high, twisting lithely along the tortured path of the river. This region plays host to a magical wonderland of springs, caves and jagged peaks. Stop at the villages of Bov, Lakatnik and Opletnya.

3 Bov

Stop at the village of Bov to find the footpath that leads to Skaklya Waterfall, one of the highest in the country. The route is very clearly marked from the railway station.

4 Lakatnik

The village has one of the country's most famous formations, the Lakatnik

Rocks – birthplace of Bulgarian mountaineering.

5 Opletnya

Opletnya is famed for its sheep's cheese and now has a plant producing Bulgarian 'yellow cheese' – the ingredient on many a Bulgarian pizza! A kilometre (²/₃ mile) beyond the village there's a turning right to the village of Elenov Dol. The Sedemte Prestola Monastery sits high in the Balkan Peaks off this road at the end of a three-hour walk.

Roads deteriorate around Zverino. 10km (6 miles) beyond Zverino you'll find a small signpost to Cherepish Monastery (left and then 500m/550yds down a track).

6 Cherepishki Manastir (Cherepish Monastery)

Cherepish is evocatively set on a narrow valley by the river in a cleft in the jagged white cliffs. It's almost invisible from the main road and it's like a world apart. Geese, ducks and piglets roam free just outside the monastery complex. Apart from the occasional sounds of road traffic it could almost be the 18th century (*see also p125*).

Returning to the road, the river valley is once again given over to agriculture. Don't stop off at Mezdra. Instead go north to Vratsa and visit one of the cafés in ul. Hristo Botev, before returning to Sofia.

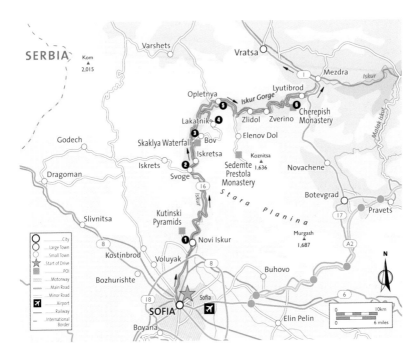

Central Bulgaria

Dominated by the eastern Balkan Mountains, also known as the Stara Planina range, central Bulgaria has always been the core of the country, both geographically and culturally. Two old Bulgarian capitals can be found here, along with a handful of traditional villages preserved as living museums, where you'll be able to stroll around some of the finest National Revival architecture in the country.

In this heartland of Bulgarian nationalism many towns proudly remember their native sons lost in the fight for freedom. The monasteries nestling in remote valleys lent their support to the nationalists but their

exceptional mural decoration is what draws non-Bulgarian tourists.

Arbanasi

One of the architectural highlights of central Bulgaria, Arbanasi is now a

village (albeit one that is home to a sizeable contingent of urban second-homers) but was once much larger; granted exemption from all taxation by Süleyman I in the 1530s, it grew wealthy from Ottoman trade. Bulgaria's upper echelons were drawn here throughout the 17th and 18th centuries, building expansive mansions, but most of these were destroyed during raids by Turkish bandits. Today the remaining buildings and a handful of the 90 churches erected in Arbanasi have been protected under Bulgarian law. Renovation work is an ongoing process, but you'll see many fine completed examples – strong stone houses and large gardens set amid high stone walls. A number of Revival buildings have been transformed into charming boutique hotels, making Arbanasi a relaxing place to stay and an alternative to the limited choice at Veliko Turnovo (*see pp70–75*).

Konstantsaliev House is an excellent National Revival mansion. The upper floors are furnished in period style with original pieces. (*No street address; open: daily 9am–6pm; admission charge.*)

Arbanasi's Rozhdesto Hristovo (Nativity) Church (*open: 9am–6pm; admission charge*) is the oldest in the town. The interior design is unusual as it features separate sections for the sexes, but the church is renowned for its decoration, including splendid murals of The Last Judgement and The Nativity, both completed in 1597, and

A picturesque well in Arbanasi

the fine iconostasis carved by master craftsmen from Tryavna (*see pp67–9*).

Archangels St Michael and Gabriel's Church in the southeast of the village was built between the mid-16th and late 18th centuries. Its murals show a development in style over the period. *5km (3 miles) northeast of Veliko Turnovo. Bus connections with Veliko Turnovo from the main road 400m (440yds) from the village.*

THE BEAUTIFUL BULGARIA PROJECT

Since the fall of communism the Bulgarian authorities have embarked on an ambitious programme to renovate the country's shabby, neglected National Revival architecture. The old quarters of many towns and villages have taken advantage of generous grants to save these beautiful buildings (*see pp26–7*).

Dryanovo Monastery

Dryanovski Manastir (Dryanovo Monastery)

Founded in the 12th century, Dryanovo is most famed for its role in the fight for Bulgarian freedom. Before the Russo-Turkish War (1877–8) it was a main hideout for the Haidouks (*see pp78–9*), including Vasil Levski, and during the war it became a battleground as local people fought with Turkish forces bent on wholesale slaughter. The Bulgarians were unsuccessful, not helped by an accidental explosion of their gunpowder stock, and many died as Ottoman forces stormed the complex. A small mausoleum at the site marks the event and the monks will point out the damage done to the Holy Archangel St Michael Church during the attack. It has undergone a major renovation to bring its frescoes back to the brilliant colours they displayed when they had just been completed.

For more background on the role of Dryanovo during the Russo-Turkish War visit the **Komplex Vodopadi** next door (*open: Mon–Fri 9am–noon & 12.30–3.30pm, Sat & Sun 9.45am–3.45pm*), where there is a small museum relating to the uprising (*admission charge*).

The Dryanovo ecotrail offers a marked walking route through the countryside around the monastery, and you can explore **Bacho Kiro Cave** (*open: daily 9am–6pm; admission charge*), one of the largest in the country. *5km (3 miles) west of the village of Dryanovo, 25km (15¹/₂ miles) southwest of Veliko Turnovo.*
www.dryanovomonastery.hit.bg.
Open: daily 7am–8pm. Free admission. Bus connections from Veliko Turnovo to the turn-off on the main road. Then a 500m (550yd) walk to the monastery.

Elena

One of the least known of Bulgaria's 'living museums', Elena possesses exceptional National Revival architecture including the **National Revival Complex** around the Church of the Assumption, a collection of 19th-century buildings (*open: daily 9am–noon & 1–5pm; admission charge*), and **Daskalolivnitsa**, the first teacher-

training complex in Bulgaria, opened in 1844, which now hosts a museum charting the development of the village (*open: daily 9am–noon & 2–5pm; admission charge*).
40km (25 miles) southeast of Veliko Turnovo. Bus connections with Sliven, Stara Zagora and Veliko Turnovo.

Emensko Defile (Emen Gorge)

Three kilometres (1³/₄ miles) long and 30m (100ft) high, Emen Gorge cuts into the Stara Planina hills on their northern side. The village of Emen itself is a typical agricultural settlement and there are no signs to the gorge. Park your car close to the old wooden bridge (take a right once you cross the river) and a

THE FREEDOM FIGHTER'S RESOLUTION

'Pasha,
We want the Government to acknowledge our rights as a people and until this is done we will not surrender to your tormentors' hands as long as we are still alive.

We have made our decision to die and we shall keep our oath.'

Rebel leader Bacho Kiro's reply when he was asked by Fazlu Pasha to surrender during the siege of Dryanovo Monastery.

footpath leads up through the fields to the gorge mouth. In a totally unspoilt ecosystem, you'll be surrounded by butterflies and crickets, along with several hundred other species of insects, as you walk along the footpath. Frogs

Central Bulgaria

The Emen Gorge in the Stara Planina Mountains

call loudly from pools gouged over the aeons by the stream running through the gorge floor, and up on the left side of the cliff at the entrance is a large cave housing a small colony of bats.
30km (18 1/2 miles) northwest of Veliko Turnovo. No feasible public transport.

Etur

Etur (often spelt Etâr or Etâra) Ethnographical Village Museum is unique in Bulgaria – a theme park, although don't let the use of that phrase conjure up a Disneyland image. This is a faithful reproduction of a 19th-century Bulgarian settlement. The wood and lime plaster buildings, with stone slab roofs in National Revival style, are linked by cobbled alleyways, rebuilt here on this expansive wooded site by the side of a fast-flowing stream.

Etur offers a full range of traditional Bulgarian arts and crafts. Over 50 workshops and studios offer the finest hand-crafted souvenirs and you can watch the craftsmen at work. You'll find artisans such as jewellers, weavers, potters, leather-toolers and glass-blowers, as well as trades including wheelwrights, cobblers and knife-sharpeners working in water-powered mills (*see p145*).
7km (4 1/2 miles) southeast of Gabrovo. Look for a turning to the left just before the road climbs to the Shipka Pass opposite the panel telling you if the pass is open. Open: daily 9am–7pm, shorter hours in winter. Admission charge, tickets valid for the day. Bus 36 from Gabrovo, then 7 or 8.

A GABROVO JOKE!

Here's an example of Gabrovo humour:
'Why are you crying?' the man asks a young child.
'Because my mother gave me a lev and I've lost it', says the boy.
'Well, here is another lev, you can stop crying now', replies the man. But the child continues to sob.
'What's the matter now?' enquires the man.
'Because if I hadn't lost the first lev, I would have had two now!' retorts the boy.

Gabrovo

This rather insignificant little town has earned a reputation as the centre of Bulgarian comedy – for reasons unknown. Its citizens are the butt of many jokes but seem to have taken it in good humour; the town even has a **Museum of Humour and Satire** (*ul. Bryanska 68; tel: (066) 807 228; www.humourhouse.bg; open: summer daily 9am–6pm; winter Mon–Sat 9am–6pm; admission charge*) where comic works from dozens of countries can be viewed. The museum also has a colourful collection of carnival masks from around the world.
47km (29 miles) north of Kazanluk. Bus connections with Kazanluk, Plovdiv, Ruse and Veliko Turnovo.

Karlovo

Birthplace of Bulgarian hero Vasil Levski (look out for a monumental statue of the man with a lion at his side in pl. Vasil Levski), Karlovo was a prosperous trading town until the

Russo-Turkish War, when it was torched by Ottoman forces.

The **Vasil Levski House-Museum** (*ul. General Kartzov 57; tel: (0335) 93489; www.vlevskimuseum-bg.org; open: daily 8.30am–1pm & 2–5pm; admission charge. Guided tours in English, separate charge*) has information in English about Levski and his life. Only the cellar of the house is original; the rest was lost to the fire of 1877 but rebuilt to the original plans in 1937.

50km (31 miles) north of Plovdiv. Bus connections with Hisar, Kazanluk, Sliven, Stara Zagora and Troyan.

Kazanluk

Kazanluk (often spelt Kazanlâk) is an unprepossessing town set between the Rodopi and Stara Planina ranges. It is famed for its **Thracian tomb**, built in the 4th century BC. Protected by UNESCO, it is often closed for archaeological study, but don't despair, as you'll find a full-scale replica of the tomb in the gardens on site (*both at Tyulbeto Park; open: daily 9am–5pm; admission charge*). The beehive-shaped dome is 12m (39ft) in diameter and decorated with fantastic murals depicting funerary rituals. The tomb is reached down an entry corridor flanked by dramatic battle friezes.

Central Bulgaria

Hisar's Roman-Byzantine remains

To complement the visit, head next to the **Iskra Museum** (*ul. Sv Kiril & Metodii; open: daily 9am–5pm; admission charge*) which exhibits frescoes from the Magli tomb – another Thracian funerary cavern – and an interesting collection of Greek artefacts found in the region.

Kazanluk's position at the eastern end of the Valley of the Roses makes it a suitable place to find the **Museum of the Roses** (*ul. Osvobozhdenie; open: daily 9am–5pm in summer; admission charge*) with displays on the techniques for manufacturing natural fragrances; however, explanations are only in Cyrillic. The shop sells some fragrant souvenirs, including rose-scented soaps, oils and perfumes.

40km (25 miles) northwest of Stara Zagora. Bus connections with Lovech, Stara Zagora and Veliko Turnovo.

Khisar (Hisar)

Known for its mineral springs, Hisar (also known as Hisarya/Хисаря) is popular with Bulgarians, who travel here for the restorative treatments (*see pp164–5*). If this isn't your thing, come to explore the remains of the ancient spa that provided curative therapies for over 1,000 years.

The immense walls are the most obvious feature of the old settlement. Built during the Roman era but fortified by the Byzantines, they stand 5m (16ft) high and are the most complete in the country. The **Archaeological Museum** (*ul.*

VALLEY OF THE ROSES

Until recently Bulgaria produced 70 per cent of the world's rose oil, a vital resource in the perfume and cosmetics industry. In the 17th century, demand for oil from Western Europe and particularly the French perfume industry hit the roof and it became Bulgaria's most important export commodity. Even today high-profile cosmetics houses such as Helena Rubinstein seek out this pure essence and you can buy Bulgarian-made rose souvenirs such as soap, oils and sweets. The modern industry is concentrated in the valley west of Kazanluk.

Stamboliiski 8; tel: (0337) 62012; open: daily 8am–noon & 1–4.30pm; admission charge) features a model of Hisar at its zenith, along with local handicrafts and traditional tools.

15km (9 1/2 miles) southwest of Karlovo. Bus connections with Karlovo, Troyan, Plovdiv and Veliko Turnovo.

Koprivshtitsa

A tour de force of Bulgarian National Revival architecture, Koprivshtitsa is a living museum set in a verdant valley in the heart of the Sredna Gora Mountains. In the 15th century this simple farming village was transformed by the arrival of the ruling nobility, who abandoned the capital Veliko Turnovo in the wake of the Ottoman invasion. They built luxurious mansions among the woodland here, creating a kind of royal court in waiting that in turn attracted the Bulgarian intellectual and the merchant elite.

It was at Koprivshtitsa that the seeds of Bulgarian discontent bore the fruit of rebellion when the national uprising was announced on Kalachev Bridge on 20 April 1876. The founding of the Bulgarian state proved a mixed blessing for the village. The merchants and intellectuals moved back to the cities, forsaking their mansions, but this has allowed Koprivshtitsa to retain its authentic architecture and its 19th-century ambience.

You'll make the best of your visit by simply wandering as the whim takes you along the cobbled alleyways, the banks of the River Topolnitsa, which runs through the heart of the town, or the several streams that feed it. A number of houses have stories to tell. **Oslekov House** (*ul. Garanilo; open: Tue–Sun 9.30am–5.30pm*) is a *pièce de résistance* of Revival style built in 1856 for a merchant who lost his life in the uprising. The rooms feature period

furniture and the paraphernalia of daily life.

Lutov House (also called Topalov House) (*ul. Nikola Belodezhdov; open: Wed–Mon 9.30am–5.30pm*) is another exceptional example, constructed in 1854, with interior frescoes depicting scenes from Venice, Cairo and Istanbul. The lower floors feature a display of articles made from locally fabricated felt, some of which are for sale.

Kableshkov House (*ul. Todor Kableshkov 8*), completed two decades later, was owned by the man responsible for firing the first shot of the uprising and now houses a museum dedicated to the struggle for independence.

Popular with Bulgarian visitors, **Debelyanov House** (*ul. Garanilo; open: Tue–Sun 9.30am–5.30pm*) is dedicated to acclaimed poet Dimcho Debelyanov,

Central Bulgaria

Koprivshtitsa village, with houses in National Revival style

who lived here before his death during World War I. Many of his original manuscripts can be viewed; however, it will be the house itself that is most interesting to non-Bulgarian visitors.

The huge equestrian statue dominating the hillside above the town is of Georgi Benkovski, leader of the rebel cavalry, who died at the hands of the Turks in 1876. There are excellent views across the valley from here. Benkovski's mansion sits just below the statue. *110km (68 1/2 miles) west of Sofia. Village open: 24 hours. Free admission. Admission charge is a combined ticket for all houses open to the public. Bus connections with Pirdop 35km (22 miles) away and minibuses from Sofia.*

Kotel

Birthplace of revolutionaries Georgi Rakovski and Safronii Vrachanski, Kotel is famed for its woollen carpets, which are still handmade on wooden looms. The **Carpet Exhibition Hall** (or Galatan School) (*ul. Izvorska 17; tel: (0453) 2316; open: Mon–Fri; summer 9am–6pm; winter 8am–noon & 1–5pm; admission charge*) has displays of traditional patterns and colours, and it also sells carpets. *50km (31 miles) northeast of Sliven. Bus connections with Sliven.*

Lovech

One of the major beneficiaries of the Beautiful Bulgaria Project (*see p55*), the old town centre of Lovech is being carefully restored with over 160 buildings already completed in the

Varosha Architectural Reserve, as the old town is known.

In the 19th century, Lovech was a hotbed of the revolutionary movement, being the central hub of Vasil Levski's national guerrilla cell network. It now plays host to the **Revival and National Liberation Movement Museum**, also known as the Vasil Levski Museum (*ul. Marin Pop Loukanov; open Tue–Sun 8am–noon & 1–5pm; admission charge*). Cobbled ul. Marin Pop Loukanov has other attractions, including an **Ethnological Museum** (*open: daily 8am–noon & 1–5pm; admission charge*) and the superb Byzantine Church of St Bogoroditsa (Church of the Holy Virgin).

You'll also want to see the Pokritiyat Most (covered bridge), with its rows of wooden shops. Designed by architect Kolyo Ficheto and originally built in 1872 (it was destroyed by fire in 1925 but was rebuilt), it is unique in Bulgaria.

The large fortress atop the hill was the place where the treaty leading to the founding of the Second Bulgarian Empire was signed. The citadel now lies in evocative ruins. *35km (22 miles) north of Troyan. Bus connections with Kazanluk, Sliven and Veliko Turnovo.*

Madara

This humble modern village is famed for the majestic bas-relief commonly called the **Madarski Konnik (Madara Horseman)** (*open: summer daily 8am–7pm; winter daily 8am–5pm; admission charge*) that is impressed into nearby cliffs. Carved in the 8th century AD to celebrate the military victories of Khan Tervel, who repelled an Arab invasion in the early years of the century and greatly expanded the territory of the First Bulgarian Empire, it features a mounted cavalryman, perhaps Tervel himself, spearing a lion.

Above the relief atop the cliffs, reached by a carved rock staircase, are the remains of the Madara Fortress, built in the 12th century to protect Bulgaria during the Second Empire (1185–1396).

15km (9 ¹/₂ miles) east of Shumen. Bus connections are poor but best from Shumen. Frequent train connections from Shumen.

Oreshak

Most people visit tiny Oreshak, renowned for the production of plum brandy, for the **Exhibition of Applied Arts and Traditional Crafts Complex** (*open: daily 9am–5pm; admission charge for craft exhibition*). Here you can see and buy a comprehensive range of local handicrafts, including ceramics, embroidery, weaving and woodcarvings. The complex hosts one of Bulgaria's most famous fairs in late August each year.

The Madara Horseman, carved into the cliff face

Oreshak plum brandy

7km (4 1/2 miles) west of Troyan. Bus connection with Troyan.

Shipka

High in the Shipchenska Planina hills, the 1,300m (4,265ft) high mountain pass at Shipka played an important role in the outcome of the Russo-Turkish War, when a force of Russian conscripts and Bulgarian volunteers repelled some 30,000 Turkish soldiers, a relief army for besieged forces further north at Pleven. Seven thousand defenders are thought to have died, considered heroes in both Bulgaria and Russia.

The major attractions here are both monuments to the lost. At the highest point along the route, atop Mount Stoletov, is the rather dour **Freedom Monument** erected in 1934 (*open: daily 9am–7pm; admission charge*), offering fantastic panoramic views over the valleys below. At the base of the pass to the south, just outside Shipka village, is the glorious, colourful **St Nikolai Church** (*open: daily 8am–5pm; admission charge*), built in 1902 in ornate Russian Orthodox style. Inside lie the remains of many of the Russian fallen – a poignant final resting place so far away from their homes.

18km (11 miles) north of Kazanluk. Bus connections with Kazanluk and Gabrovo.

Shumen

The **Shumen Fortress** (*open: summer daily 8.30am–6pm; winter daily 8.30am–5pm; admission charge*), on the plateau overlooking the town and the valley, is Shumen's main tourist attraction. More than a simple citadel, its first walls were erected as early as the Iron Age (*c.* 8th century BC) and expanded under the Thracians and the Romans to house a whole community. Utilised by the Byzantines, it became a Bulgarian stronghold during the Second Empire, forming a pivotal cog in the country's protective shield. There's a model in the History Museum showing how the fort looked at its zenith. When Ottoman forces finally breached the walls the fortress's mighty defences were systematically neutralised, and later the stone was taken for other buildings in the town. Today the remains are an evocative place to explore, especially for lovers of castles and citadels. A maze of stout square buildings indicates where homes, shops and storerooms once stood. There's little explanation at the site, though the ticket office does have a rather old book on the history of the fort with a page in English.

On the range of hills across the valley and in clear sight of the fortress is the colossal **Monument to the Founders of the Bulgarian State** (*open: summer daily 8.30am–6pm; winter daily 8.30am–5pm; admission charge*), erected in 1981 to commemorate the first Bulgarian Empire. From a distance it looks like a series of immense concrete blocks abandoned when a building project came to a halt. But close up, the series of titanic stone statues depicting the military heroes of the Bulgarian Empire, including a stylised Madara Horseman

(*see p62*), has an immense power and masculine beauty. In another section of the monument, modern mosaics chart the influence of religion.

Despite its rather grey mantle, Shumen itself has a couple of attractions to visit. The **Sherif Halil Pasha Mosque** (*open: daily 9am–6pm; admission charge*), known locally as the Tombul or Fat Mosque because of the shape of its huge dome, is said to be the largest mosque in the country still in use. Built in 1744, it is highly decorated. The **History Museum** (*bul. Slavyanski 17; open: Mon–Fri 9am–5pm; admission charge*) has one of the best collections in central Bulgaria, being particularly strong in Thracian artefacts and Roman finds from Veliki Preslav (*see p69*).

Shumen Fortress has guarded the valley since the 8th century BC

15km (9 1/2 miles) north of Veliki Preslav. Bus connections with Burgas, Dobrich, Ruse and Veliko Turnovo.

Sliven

Set amid the eastern Balkan Mountains' peaks, Sliven was the major hiding place of the Haidouks (*see pp78–9*), the Bulgarian rebels who waged a guerrilla war against the Turks throughout the 18th and 19th centuries, precipitating the Bulgarian Uprising. They survived for decades in the seemingly impenetrable Blue Rocks (*see p137*), now a national park where a chairlift whisks you with ease to the caves used as homes by the revolutionaries.

The town's **History Museum** (*ul. Tsar Osvoboditel 18; open: daily 9am–noon & 1–5pm; admission charge*) predictably concentrates on the Haidouk story, displaying artefacts connected with the rebel action. It also displays a range of ancient finds excavated in the area but doesn't have captions in English.

The **Hadzhi Dimitur House-Museum** (*ul. Assenova 2; open: daily Mon–Fri 9am–noon & 2–5pm; admission charge*) has a section dedicated to Hadzhi Dimitur, a leader of the rebel movement, but comprises several interesting 19th-century National Revival structures, including an old inn and ensemble of farm buildings.

69km (43 miles) northeast of Stara Zagora. Bus connections with Karlovo, Plovdiv, Stara Zagora and Veliko Turnovo.

Stara Zagora

Although Stara Zagora lies on ancient foundations dating back to Thracian times, the city was razed by the Turks in 1877, an action that destroyed many magnificent Thracian, Roman and Byzantine remains. However, among the town's verdant avenues there are still some treasures to be found, including the Roman theatre on ul. Mitropolit, the forum on bul. Bishop Methodii Kousev, and mosaics on the floor of the main post office and on ul. General Stoletov.

Even more ancient are the 8,000-year-old houses at the **Neolithic Dwellings Museum** on Bereketska Mogila (*off bul. Dr Todor Stoyanovich; open: Tue–Sat 9am–1pm & 1.30–5.30pm; admission charge*), the largest and best preserved of such finds in Europe. The important discernible finds can be viewed in a separate gallery along with artefacts from other sites in the region.

33km (21 miles) southeast of Kazanluk. Bus connections to Burgas, Kazanluk, Plovdiv, Sliven and Veliko Turnovo.

Troyanski Manastir (Troyan Monastery)

Troyan is the third-largest monastery in Bulgaria. Founded as late as the 16th century, it was badly damaged in several Turkish attacks during the 17th and 18th centuries and much was rebuilt during the expansion of the complex during the 1830s. It was at Troyan, always a hotbed of pro-

Bulgarian activities, that Vasil Levski (*see pp78–9*) finalised his new method of warfare – small, mobile guerrilla cells that proved a real thorn in the side of the Ottoman forces.

The monastery is renowned for its wood decoration, the highest-quality hand carving by masters from Tryavna (*see below*). The revered Three-Handed Holy Virgin icon is its most precious possession, though this is only unveiled during the Assumption celebrations on 15 August. The Church of the Holy Virgin, which houses the icon, was built in 1835 with murals by master artist Zahari Zograf, though many are difficult to see because of soot deposits from the votive candles.

During the Bulgarian National Revival period the village of Troyan was renowned for its crafts. Today there seems little evidence of a living industry, but it has a worthwhile **Museum of Applied Art and Crafts** (*pl. Vuzhrazhdane; tel: (0670) 22063; open: daily 9am–5pm; admission charge*) with excellent displays of high-quality ceramics, weaving and woodcarving. *Monastery 10km (6 miles) east of Troyan village. Bus connection with Troyan village; connections from Troyan to Karlovo, Plovdiv and Veliko Turnovo.*

Tryavna

One of the architectural highlights of Bulgaria, Tryavna is one of a handful of living museums (others include Elena and Koprivshtitsa): a village seemingly left behind in the 19th century, a microcosm of all that is good in the Bulgarian National Revival style (*see pp26–7*). The village was at the centre of the arts and crafts movement

Troyan Monastery dates from the 16th century

Central Bulgaria

Tryavna's historic clock tower

of the time, being particularly famed for its woodcarving. The artisans of Tryavna – graduates of the Tryavna School as it became known – were in high demand throughout the Balkans and Russia in the late 1800s. Today it is still a thriving artists' colony.

Tryavna is the least busy of the living museum villages and it's much easier to take in the detail as you stroll around.

A good place to start is the main square in town, pl. Kapitan Dyado Nikola. Flanked by an ensemble of fine 19th-century buildings, it offers one of the best vistas in central Bulgaria. **St Archangel Michael's Church** (*open: daily 7am–6pm*) sits on the square. Originally medieval (Second Bulgarian Empire), it was rebuilt in 1819 in the

same style when the original edifice was set alight by the Turks. The interior is decorated with exceptional Tryavna School carvings. **Staroto Shkolo** (*pl. Kapitan Dyado Nikola 7; tel: (0677) 2517; open: daily 9am–5pm; admission charge*), built in 1836, was the village school but has now been tastefully renovated to host an eclectic collection of ancient and modern art. The permanent collection is by contemporary artist Dimitar Kazakov and sculptor Zlatko Paunov, but they are juxtaposed by the displays of 19th-century objects used in the school.

From the square it's a short walk across the diminutive stone bridge to ul. Slaveikov, an exceptional cobbled street flanked by numerous noteworthy mansions. Visit **Daskalov House** (*ul.

Slaveikov 27; tel: (0677) 2166; open: daily 10am–7pm; admission charge) for a collection of high-quality woodcarving from the Tryavna School. The house itself has some fine carved detail. At No 45 you'll find **Totyu Gabenski Picture Gallery** (*tel: (0677) 2166; open: Mon–Fri 9am–1pm & 2–6pm; admission charge, tickets at Daskalov House*), an 1830s mansion displaying over 500 works by Bulgarian artists, including Troyan native Totyu Gabenski.

Other interesting buildings are the **Tryavna School of Icon Painting** (*ul. Breza 1; tel: (0677) 3753; open: 10am–6pm; admission charge*) and the 1805 **Angel Kanchev House** (*ul. Angel Kanchev; tel: (0677) 2398; open: Tue–Sat summer 8am–6pm; winter 9am– 4.30pm*), home of the eponymous freedom fighter, which hosts a retrospective on his role in the independence movement.
45km (28 miles) southwest of Veliko Turnovo. Bus connections with Gabrovo.

Veliki Preslav

Founded in 821 by Khan Omurtag, Veliki Preslav (Great Preslav) became Bulgaria's original capital when the First Empire was proclaimed under Tsar Simeon. At that time it was one of the most important cities in Europe, a hub of transport, trade and politics, but it suffered in the constant friction between Bulgaria and the Byzantines and was razed by the Turks when they rampaged across the country in 1388.

The extensive ruins of the old capital are fascinating for those who like their history unexcavated and unmanicured. They extend over 5sq km (2sq miles) – wear comfortable shoes – and you'll be able to explore the public baths, the workshop district and the remains of the old ramparts. The core of the city was the ancient walled citadel containing the old Royal Palace and the remains of churches, storehouses and bath complexes.
2km (1¼ miles) south of modern Preslav. Open: 24 hours. Free admission; guided tours in English, separate charge – contact the Archaeological Museum.

Mosaic of Sts Cyril and Methodius in Veliki Preslav Archaeological Museum

The **Archaeological Museum** (*adjacent to the ruins; open: daily summer 9am–6pm; winter 9am–5pm; admission charge*) displays a vast range of artefacts harvested from the site. Mundane items include pottery and tools; however, there are also treasures, including a stunning gold necklace and the old royal seals.

20km (12 1/2 miles) southwest of Shumen. Bus connections with Shumen.

Veliko Turnovo

'City of the Tsars', Veliko Turnovo (also spelt Veliko Târnovo), meaning Great Turnovo, witnessed many of the pivotal moments in Bulgarian history. Capital of the country during the Second Empire (1185–1396), when it was second in importance only to Constantinople, it rose again during the National Revival period. In fact the Bulgarian state was proclaimed and the constitution written here following the departure of the Turks. However, it lost out to Sofia when a new capital of the post-Ottoman Bulgaria was chosen.

The town's setting is spectacular. Surrounded by mountain peaks and cut by the deep sinuous gorge of the River Yantra, the dramatic Tsarevets and Trapezitsa hills bear down on the magnificent old town, which clings limpet-like to the sheer valley sides. The streets seemingly drape themselves one below the other, forming one of the most photogenic vistas in Bulgaria.

Evocative remains of the old capital of Veliki Preslav, once a major European city

Veliko Turnovo clings to the Tsarevets hillside

The hills have been settled since the Neolithic period and Tsarevets forms a natural fortress which has been enhanced by man throughout the generations. First Thracians and then Romans fortified the hill, but when the Byzantines arrived in the 5th century AD they made it a key citadel in their defences and it formed the heart of the Second Empire capital – then called Turnovgrad. Today, the **Tsarevets Fortress** is one of Bulgaria's most impressive tourist attractions (*tel: (062) 638 841; open: daily summer 8am–7pm; winter 9am–5pm; admission charge*). Though large sections are little more than piles of rubble, the result of a final sacking by the Turks in 1393, the citadel once supported a population of thousands. The Patriarch's Complex sitting at the highest point on the hill has been restored and features a series

of modern murals relating turning points in Bulgaria's history. Just below to the north is the Royal Palace and further north still the noblemen's quarters. To the south, on a precipitous crag, is Baldwin's tower, where the Byzantine emperor Baldwin was imprisoned before his execution in 1205.

An impressive evening sound-and-light show takes place at all times of year provided there is enough demand (*for information tel: (062) 636 952 or 0885 080865*). The show is easily visible from many quarters of the town, so it isn't limited to ticket holders.

From the fort you'll get dramatic views of the old town, which is one of the finest in Bulgaria. The streets are a treasure trove of National Revival buildings, many the work of one architect, Kolyo Ficheto. As with other

National Revival house, Veliko Turnovo

Bulgarian towns and villages, one simply has to stroll around to soak in the architectural detail. Though many buildings are in the process of being renovated, there are also a number in desperate need of tender loving care. Most are not open to the public.

Two of the town's major museums relate to the founding of the Third Empire but, with little explanation except in Cyrillic, are of limited interest to non-Bulgarian speakers. The **Museum of National Revival and Constituent Assembly** (*ul. Ivan Vazov; tel: (062) 629 821; open: Wed–Mon 9am–6pm; admission charge*) is housed in the building where the first parliament of the free Bulgaria met to adopt the new constitution, and the **Museum of Contemporary Bulgarian History** (*ul. Tchtalischa; open: Tue–Sun 9am–5pm; admission charge*) retraces

the period of the Revolution with armaments, uniforms and old photographs of the time. Far more worthwhile is the **Archaeological Museum** (*ul. Ivan Vazov; tel: (062) 634 946; open: Tue–Sun 9am–6pm, Mon noon–6pm; admission charge*) which contains some excellent Second Empire artefacts from Tsarevets fortress and a large collection of Roman artefacts from nearby Nikopolis ad Istrum (*see p77*) and beyond.

The glorious setting of the **State Art Gallery** (*Assenovtsi Park; tel: (062) 638 941; open: Tue–Sun 10am–6pm; admission charge; guided tour in English, separate charge*), on the point of a sinuous curve in the river, is perhaps more inviting than the collection, which is limited to local artists. Overlooking the river in front of the gallery is the dramatic **Monument of the Assens**, erected to commemorate the founding of the Second Bulgarian Empire. There are excellent views over the old town from here.

Sarafkina House (*ul. Gurko 88; open: Mon–Fri 9am–5.30pm; admission charge*) is worth a visit. Constructed in 1861 for a wealthy Turkish merchant, it houses a bijou but interesting Ethnographical Museum. The upper floor looks as if the family could still be living there, with genuine 19th-century interior design and furniture; there are even family photos on the walls.

Veliko Turnovo has numerous churches. The large **cathedral** (*ul. Ivan Vazov*) was designed by Ficheto in 1872, as was St Spas Church, which was abandoned after an earthquake in 1913. **The Church of St Peter and St Paul** (*ul. Mitropolska; tel: (062) 638 841; open: hours vary; free admission*) features some fine murals, the earliest from the 14th century. The **Forty Martyrs Church** (*ul. Mitropolska; open: daily 9.30am–6pm; admission charge*) is the most interesting church in the town, however. Built in 1230 during the Second Empire, it became a royal mausoleum before being converted into a mosque during the Ottoman era. Today it houses a library of rare manuscripts. On the outskirts of town on the route to Arbanasi (*see pp54–5*) is the **Church of St Dimitar** (*ul. Patriarch Evtimii; open daily 9am–noon & 1–6pm; admission charge*). It was at the consecration of the church in 1185 that Tsars Assen and Petar declared the uprising that would eventually lead to the founding of the Second Bulgarian Empire.

46km (28 1/2 miles) northeast of Gabrovo. Bus connections with Shumen, Gabrovo and Stara Zagora. Train station with connections to Pleven, Plovdiv, Ruse, Sofia, Stara Zagora and Varna.
Tourist office: ul. Hristo Botev.
Tel: (062) 622 148. Open: Mon–Fri 9am–noon & 1–6pm.

The State Art Gallery and Assens Monument

Walk: Old Veliko Turnovo

Veliko Turnovo is one of Bulgaria's main tourist destinations. In addition to the famous fortress on Tsarevets hill, there are several churches and many Bulgarian National Revival buildings which are well worth seeing. The old part of town spreads over three hills.

Starting from the Tsarevets Fortress, this 5km (3-mile) walk takes about 3 hours.

1 Krepostta Tsarevets (Tsarevets Fortress)

This ruined citadel was the engine room of the Second Bulgarian Empire. However, the most impressive remains today are the crenellated boundary walls and the renovated Patriarch's Complex with its distinctive belfry.

Walk away from the fortress on ul. Ivan Vazov. After a couple of minutes on the left you'll find the major museum complexes of the town.

2 Museums

The Museum of National Revival and Constituent Assembly is housed in the old neoclassical Town Hall. Next door is the Archaeological Museum, and behind this stands the Museum of Contemporary Bulgarian History.

From the museums walk straight ahead, keeping the Church of Konstantin and Elena (1872) on your right. This brings you to ul. Gurko.

3 Ul. Gurko

Cobbled ul. Gurko is a typical 19th-century street with mansions with overhanging closed balconies. To the left you can look down the canyon to the State Art Gallery in Assenovtsi Park.

4 Sarafkina Kushta (Sarafkina House)

At 88 ul. Gurko you'll find Sarafkina House, constructed in 1861 for a banking family. The collection of furniture and other pieces inside re-creates its 19th-century splendour.

At the end of ul. Gurko climb up to the parallel street, the major arterial route through the town (this changes its name as it travels east to west). Cross the street and take the flight of steps up into the Varosha district of town. The steps terminate at ul. Mednikarska. Walk straight across up ul. Slaveikov and then turn right when you reach ul. Kiril & Metodii.

5 Sts Cyril and Methodius Church

Here on the corner you'll find the Church of Sts Cyril and Methodius, erected in 1861 with money donated by architect Kolyo Ficheto.

Turn right down ul. Kiril & Metodii and then right down ul. Shipka to find St Nikolai Church on the left.

6 St Nikolai Church

Erected in 1836, this church was Ficheto's apprentice piece.

Walk down past the church then left and right to reach the main arterial route again. Turn right here and follow the road until you reach the junction with ul. Hristo Botev (approximately 1km/²⁄₃ mile) where you'll take another left turn.

Walk past the tourist office on your left. When you reach the junction with ul. Stamboliiski turn left and walk down the street to Stambolov Most, the iron bridge over the Yantra Gorge. Cross the bridge into Assenovtsi Park.

7 Assenovtsi Park

At the northwestern tip of the promontory stands the huge *Monument to the Assens*. This is a truly heroic creation, depicting a chariot being drawn by two horses in full flight. The State Art Gallery in the centre of the park boasts an immense collection of over 4,000 pieces. The museum has a café and terrace where you can enjoy the breathtaking natural landscapes.

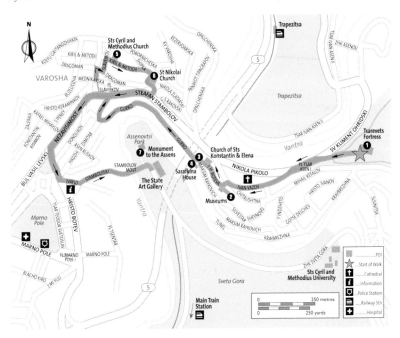

Drive: Touring the Veliko Turnovo countryside

Veliko Turnovo makes an excellent base from which to tour. Within a 30-minute radius of the town there is a varied range of attractions to keep the most fussy tourists happy, from ancient Roman remains and National Revival villages to Bulgarian wineries. This drive covers 65km (40 miles) and should take about 4 hours excluding stops.

Leave Veliko Turnovo on the A4/E772 road east in the direction of Varna. After 10km (6 miles) take the left turn which veers towards the village of Lyaskovets.

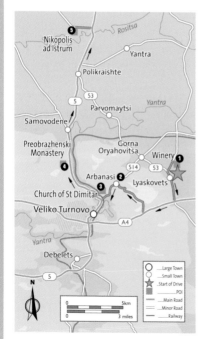

1 Lyaskovets

Surrounded by vines, this village has at its heart one of the best wine houses in Bulgaria. Visits to the Lyaskovets Winery and wine tours can be arranged but this must be done in advance (best through the tourist office in Veliko Turnovo). *Return to the main road and take a right turn back towards Veliko Turnovo. After 5km (3 miles) turn right off the road to Arbanasi.*

2 Arbanasi

Arbanasi is one of the architectural highlights of central Bulgaria, a settlement founded in the 16th century that attracted the upper classes of Bulgarian society in the National Revival period. There are excellent churches and mansions to explore, and also a selection of pretty restaurants. *Return towards Veliko Turnovo on the Veliko Turnovo/Byala road (travel on out of the other side of Arbanasi, not the way you came in). This leads downhill towards Veliko Turnovo, offering excellent views of the Tsarevets Fortress and the river. Just before you enter the town, as the castle takes your attention, you'll see a small church on the right.*

3 Tsurkvata Sveti Dimitur (Church of St Dimitar)

This is the Church of St Dimitar, the oldest church in the town. It was here during its consecration in 1185 that the Tsars declared an uprising against Byzantine domination that brought about the Second Bulgarian Empire.
Continue on over the river and into Veliko Turnovo. At the top of the hill take a right turn in the direction of Ruse (Pyce). After 8km (5 miles) look for a sign left to Preobrazhenski Monastery. The access road (around 2.5km/1¹/₂ miles) is rough but passable.

4 Preobrazhenski Manastir (Preobrazhenski Monastery)

This monastery was once one of the most powerful in the area, but today it's an evocative backwater set on a steep slope surrounded by woodland. Destroyed by the Turks, it was rebuilt during the 19th century. The diminutive Church of the Transfiguration is decorated both inside and out with exceptional murals, including Zahari Zograf's *Circle of Life* on the outside south wall (*open: daily dawn–dusk*).
From the monastery continue towards Ruse (left at the junction of the main road from the monastery link road). After 10km (6 miles) look for a signpost to the village of Nikyup/Nikjup (if you cross the river you have gone too far). Just outside the village you'll find the remains of Nikopolis ad Istrum.

5 Nikopolis ad Istrum

Nikopolis ad Istrum was a Roman colonial town founded in AD 102 and named by Emperor Trajan in commemoration of his victory over the Dacians. The best-preserved section of the city, which was destroyed by barbarians in the 6th century, is the forum, but you can view excavated streets and the low walls of houses and shops.
Return to the main road and turn right to return to Veliko Turnovo.

Preobrazhenski Monastery lies in one of the gorges of the Yantra River

The Haidouks

Throughout the 15th to the 17th centuries the Bulgarian state was brought to a state of collapse by the weight of Ottoman rule. Deprived of the ability to form political institutions, the Bulgarians found it difficult to organise any mass resistance. The Haidouks were the most successful and best known of the many locally based resistance fighters. Haidouks were fighters who left their homes to live in the mountains and woods, particularly in the Blue Rocks (*see p137*), sustaining the morale of the population but also the cause of many bloody reprisals as innocent villagers paid for Haidouk raids.

Over their long fight for freedom, the movement developed a sophisticated *modus operandi*, particularly under the guidance of Vasil Levski. This culminated in the April Uprising of 1876, when several regions rose up against the Turks. In itself the uprising was unsuccessful. Only the population of central Bulgaria rose with the rebels, following a call to arms in Koprivshtitsa in 1876, and many were slaughtered to the last man in bloody battles – the worst at Batak. But it was the Ottoman reaction to this uprising that caused Russia to come to the defence of the Bulgarians – starting the Russo-Turkish War that marked the end of Ottoman rule in Bulgaria.

Statue to Stefan Karadzha

HAIDOUK LEADERS
Vasil Levski (1837–73)
Leader of the revolutionary forces, Levski (born Vasil Kunchev, he was given the *nom de guerre* 'Levski' or

'lion') trained as a monk but turned freedom fighter in 1862. His main success was in transforming the intellectual debate for freedom into an armed struggle by setting up numerous fighting or resistance cells (called *cheti*) throughout the country, operating free of any larger colonial influence. He often set up cells in monasteries – it is said that at Troyan (*see pp66–7*) he even tried to persuade the monks to join the rebel force. He was arrested in 1872 and executed in Sofia.

Stefan Karadzha (1840–68)

Leader of a Levski *cheta*. He fought through the Balkan Mountains before being killed by the Turks. His *cheta* fought to the last man.

Georgi Benkovski (1843–76)

Successor to Levski, Benkovski hoped to introduce a system of government similar to those found in the revolutionary states of America and France.

Hristo Botev (1848–76)

One of the principal figures in the April Uprising, the poet Botev had just returned from exile in Romania in April 1876, travelling across the Danube on a seized Austrian packet boat. He was caught by the Turks and executed less than a month later.

Shipka Pass monument

Georgi Sava Rakovski (1821–67)

Early leader of the revolutionary movement, he organised the first formal armed groups to oppose the Ottoman Empire from a base in Belgrade. His dream of a Bulgarian army was never fulfilled in his lifetime.

Lyuben Karavlov (*c.* 1834–79)

Karavlov was the only revolutionary leader who lived to see an independent Bulgaria, dying in 1879.

Southwest Bulgaria

Three major mountain ranges shape the character of southwest Bulgaria. The Rila, Pirin and Rodopi ranges offer outstanding landscapes, from vertiginous peaks and high-altitude freshwater lakes to alpine meadows. Their most remote corners provide exceptional habitats for a range of creatures, particularly birds, and they also offer a year-round playground for human beings, with excellent summer hiking and winter sports opportunities.

Heartland of the ancient Thracians, the region has seen the dusty footprints of many peoples cross its land throughout recorded time. There's much here for the history lover to enjoy.

Bachkovski Manastir (Bachkovo Monastery)

Bachkovo was founded in 1083 by Georgian aristocrats Gregory and Abasi Bakuriani, who were commanders in the Byzantine army of Alexis I. It developed into a major religious complex during the Second Bulgarian Empire before being sacked by the Turks. The monastery recovered during the 17th century and today is the second richest and most influential in the country after Rila.

The approach road to the complex is flanked by souvenir stands, but these can be bypassed by parking just outside the monastery gates (parking charge).

Inside the walls, the large courtyard contains two churches. The 17th-century Church of the Assumption houses a miraculous silver icon of the Virgin, brought from Georgia in the 14th century, which is one of the most revered in Bulgaria, and a magnificent iconostasis. Unfortunately, the murals of the inner chamber have gathered a coating of soot from the votive candles and are difficult to see. The antechamber and outer gallery have brighter images.

Bachkovo Monastery

The smaller 12th-century Archangel Church is decorated with exceptional 18th-century murals by Bulgarian Renaissance master artist Zahari Zograf. The St Nikolas Chapel (often closed) contains more murals by Zograf, including a worthy *Doomsday*, while the former refectory has an exceptional painted ceiling. The small museum on site contains a collection of icons, and you can also see the 11th-century ossuary outside the complex on the far side of the car park.

30km (18 ¹/₂ miles) south of Plovdiv. Open: daily 7am–8pm. Free admission. Guided tours, with separate charge. Bus connections from Asenovgrad, which can in turn be reached from Plovdiv.

Bansko

Bansko is probably the country's premiere ski resort. Founded in the 15th century, in the midst of the Pirin Mountains, the town made money from the cultivation of tobacco and from its traditional crafts. It flourished during the National Revival when the so-called Bansko School of artists earned an international reputation. However, since the year 2000 millions of euros have been invested in winter sports facilities to ensure that the town rivals Borovets, and this in turn has been followed by several new 'alpine'-style hotels that are bringing European skiers in their droves.

Bansko has long been a popular destination for Bulgarians. It makes

A street in Bansko

the perfect base for touring the wilds of the Pirin National Park during the summer, and the town itself has over 150 officially recognised cultural monuments. Many of the old mansions are now being converted into galleries and restaurants, so it's a great town for a relaxed stroll.

The clock tower in the grounds of the **Sveta Troitsa (Holy Trinity) Church** (*pl. Vazhrazhdane*) can be seen from most parts of the old town. The interior has carved wood decoration by the master Velyan Ognev and murals by the Bansko School. From here it's a short walk to all the major museums.

Velyanov House (*ul. Velyan Ognev 5; tel: (07443) 4181; open Mon–Fri 9am–noon & 2–5pm; admission charge*) is a 17th-century mansion owned by the carving master, worth seeing for its excellent murals and decorative wood ceilings.

Museum Nikola Vaptsarov (*pl. Nikola Vaptsarov 3; tel: (07433) 3038; open: Mon–Fri 8am–noon & 2–6pm; admission charge*) displays an interesting collection of artefacts tracing Bansko's history and development. The main building of the museum was the family mansion of the Vaptsarov family. Vaptsarov himself was a poet but also a war hero and fervent anti-fascist who was executed by the wartime Bulgarian regime. The annexe contains a quality arts and crafts gallery where many items are for sale.

The town also has an **Icon Exhibition** (*ul. Sandinski 3; tel: (07443) 4005; open: Mon–Fri 9am–noon & 2–5pm; admission charge*) that displays a collection predominantly comprising 19th-century examples.

At the top of the town the gondola links Bansko to the winter ski runs or summer walking/hiking routes. It offers exceptional views of the mountains and the valley between the Pirin and Rila mountain ranges.
60km (37 miles) southeast of Blagoevgrad. Bus connections with Blagoevgrad, Plovdiv and Sofia. Tourist information pl. Nikola Vaptsarov. Tel: (07443) 8374. Open: Mon–Fri 9am–1pm & 2–5pm.

Batak

Bulgarians come to Batak to enjoy the summer activities of the nearby Batak Lake set among the western Rodopi Mountains, but the town is infamous in

Bulgarian history for the massacre of over 5,000 townspeople by the Turks during the uprising of 1876. It was this incident above all others that caused Russia to declare war on the Ottoman Empire, a bitter conflict that brought about the end of Turkish rule.

The **Church of Sveta Nedelya** (*open: Tue–Sat 9am–noon & 2–6pm; admission charge*) still bears witness to the final fate of over 2,000 townsfolk taking refuge here during the Battle of Batak. Bullet holes riddle the walls and a few damaged skulls rest in an open tomb. The town's **History Museum** (*pl. Osvodozhenie; tel: (03553) 2339; open: daily 8.30am–5pm; admission charge*) also has some moving displays on the atrocity.

60km (37 miles) southwest of Plovdiv. Bus connection with Plovdiv.

Blagoevgrad

The university town of Blagoevgrad is a lively and relatively sophisticated city, full of bars and restaurants. The centre of town, mostly pedestrianised, has pavement cafés and bars serving food, while for cultural attractions it is a short walk across the river to the old part of town called Varosha.

Varosha is an area of cobbled streets and traditional buildings that date back to the 19th century. Here you will find the Church of the Annunciation of the Virgin, its exterior characterised by red and white stripes and murals decorating the portico. The folksy-looking Kristo Hotel is directly above the church and its spacious restaurant looks down on the cobbled courtyard.

100km (62 miles) south of Sofia. Bus connections with Bansko and Sofia.

Tobacco crops drying at Blagoevgrad

Borovets

In the heart of the Rila Mountains, Borovets is a major international winter resort (*see pp100–101*) and summer hiking base. The town itself is tiny, being little more than a collection of modern hotels and associated cafés, restaurants, souvenir stalls and nightclubs, but it offers a superb setting, surrounded by peaks swathed in verdant pine forests.

*84km (52 miles) southeast of Sofia.
Bus connections with Samokov.*

Melnik

Capital of Bulgarian wine (*see pp172–3*), Melnik sits in the very far southwestern corner of the country, close to the Greek border. Set in a sheltered sandy valley, its local soils and Mediterranean climate are excellent for vines.

During the 13th century the region became the personal fiefdom of Alexei Slav. He reigned for only a short time but the remnants of several fortresses and monasteries are a legacy of his rule. The town was one of the wealthiest in the country in the late 19th century by virtue of the wine and tobacco trade, but it remained under Ottoman control until 1912, losing markets in the newly independent Bulgaria. Its population has dwindled to a fraction of its peak after a fire destroyed much of the town during the Balkan Wars (1912–13). It is officially Bulgaria's smallest town, with fewer than 400 inhabitants, but it possesses a number of well-renovated National Revival mansions and plenty of evocative ruins. Visitors also come to see the strange natural rock formations in the nearby cliffs – erosion has produced surreal shapes such as chimneys and columns.

It's best to park the car at the bottom of the village by the main road, as there are no tarmac roads to

The Borovets winter resort is ideal for skiing

Now village-sized, Melnik was once a thriving commercial town

the houses. From the main thoroughfare beside the stream, narrow alleyways lead up the hillsides to the main attractions.

The wine theme starts at **Kordopoulov Kashta (House)** (*tel: (07437) 265; open: daily 8.30am–noon & 1.30–6pm; admission charge*). Built in 1754 for a wealthy wine merchant, it is said to be one of the largest National Revival buildings in the country, with a labyrinth of hand-hewn cellars/caves for wine storage.

You can taste and buy the robust Melnik wines at **Mitko Manolev Wineries** (*tel: (0887) 545 795; open: daily 9am–midnight*). There are tables set out in a cool cave where the wine is stored or out on the small terrace that offers excellent views across the rooftops. There are several wine bars on the main street to enjoy the odd glass

or two. **Damianitza Winery** offers tasting and wine tours but it's best to book ahead (*www.damianitza.bg*).

Visit the tiny **History Museum** (*open: daily 9am–noon & 2–6pm; admission charge*) for some fascinating photographs of Melnik as a lively metropolis 100 years ago. It also features an extensive collection of local handicrafts.

Dominating the heights above the town is the Fortress of Alexei Slav, built in the 13th century. Bolyarskata Kashta, the home of the Slav family (not to be confused with the race of people called Slavs), was built in the 10th century and there are good views over the village from here, but both structures now lie in ruins.

80km (50 miles) south of Blagoevgrad. Bus connections with Blagoevgrad and Sandinski.

Traditional farming at Melnik

Pamporovo

Pamporovo, Bulgaria's most upmarket ski resort (*see pp100–101*), sits in the heart of the Rodopi Mountains. It now serves as a summer destination with beautiful surroundings of spruce and pine forest. It's also one of the most expensive places to stay outside the capital.

Pamporovo takes its name from the mule trains (*pampor*) that used to run through the high pass from Smolyan during the Ottoman era. Its first accommodation was opened in 1933.

16km (10 miles) north of Smolyan. Bus connections with Chepelare, Plovdiv and Smolyan. Tourist office near Hotel Perelik. www.pamporovo.net

Pazardzhik

Established by the Turks after the Crimean War, Pazardzhik developed quickly into one of the most important commercial towns in the eastern Ottoman Empire. It remained a mainly Muslim settlement until the 1960s, but lost all influence during the Third Bulgarian Empire and communist rule. Today, perhaps because of its association with hated Turkish rule, the town has become inextricably linked throughout Bulgaria with thievery and scams, a reputation that the evidence shows is largely undeserved, though the town does have its fair share of pickpockets, and some caution is advised.

Renowned Bulgarian artist Stanislav Dospevski (1826–76) was a native of the town. The house where he was born (*bul. Maria Luisa 54; open: Mon–Fri 9am–noon & 2–5.30pm; admission charge*) is now dedicated to the artist, preserving his personal effects and displaying several of his pieces.

More are on display in the **Stanislav Dospevski Gallery** (*pl. Konstantin Velichkov 15; open: Mon–Fri 9am–noon & 1–5pm; admission charge*), which offers a more comprehensive collection of his art and sculpture.

The two main religions also have fine edifices. The **Kurshum Dzhamiya** (mosque), built in 1667, is one of the largest in Bulgaria, while the **Sveta Bogoroditsa Cathedral**, in archetypal National Revival style, was erected to mark the foundation of the Third Bulgarian Empire. Its wooden iconostasis carved by the Debur School is unique in Bulgaria.

113km (70 miles) southeast of Sofia. Train connections with Sofia and Plovdiv. Bus connections with Batak, Sofia and Plovdiv.

Plovdiv

Plovdiv is Bulgaria's second-largest city. The site, set on several low hills on the banks of the Maritza River, has been settled for millennia as it sits at the junction of two ancient trade routes – the motorways of their day. Plovdiv has thrived through every era of the country's long and complicated history, and it is here of all places that different strands of time can be seen lying cheek by jowl. The city's many treasures deserve at least a couple of days to explore fully.

The antecedents of today's Plovdiv can be traced back to the Thracians. They fortified the site as early as 5000 BC. Philip II of Macedonia captured the Thracian town, known as Eumolpias, in 341 BC. He renamed the

Plovdiv sits in a superb hilly location

Southwest Bulgaria

Plovdiv's Roman amphitheatre

city Philipopolis and greatly expanded the complex. Under Roman rule the town was named Trimontium and then renamed again during the First Bulgarian Empire. Plovdiv was badly damaged during the Ottoman invasion but was rebuilt by the Turks, who called it Philibe. It flourished again following independence, when it developed a unique form of architecture, incorporating elements of Baroque and National Revival design, now seen both restored and in ruins in the magnificent old town.

The oldest extant ruins are the remains of Thracian Eumolpias that perch atop 200m (656ft) high Nebet Tepe (Nebet Hill). Though there's little to see apart from remnants of what were once immense walls, the hill offers good views across the rest of the city.

The Romans left a few traces (though sadly many were destroyed in later conflicts). The most bizarre are the excavated remains of a Roman stadium (the curved seats of the eastern end) that lie in an open city underpass with the concrete pillars of modern buildings resting on their marble terraces. The most impressive Roman site is without doubt the **Amphitheatre** (*ul. Hemus/ul. Tsar Ivailo; open: daily 9am–5pm; admission charge*), built during the reign of Emperor Trajan in the 2nd century AD. The structure lay underground until 1972, probably buried as the result of an earthquake, and was only rediscovered by accident. It has since been rather over-restored and now plays host to opera and folk events during the summer. The most disappointing remains have to be the scant sections of the forum (though the rest must lie underneath the main post office).

Religious buildings illustrate the period of Ottoman rule. Many Byzantine churches were destroyed in the Turkish invasion and so the city's churches are normally 16th- or 17th-century buildings resting on earlier foundations. **Sts Konstantin and Elena** (*ul. Saborna 24; open: daily 8am–6pm*) is the oldest, tracing its history back to the 4th century, though the current church dates from the 1830s. The highlights are the gilded iconostasis and collection of icons. The **Sveta Nedelya Church** (*ul. Slaveikov 40; tel: (032) 623 270; open: daily 8am–5pm*) was erected in 1578 and should be visited for the walnut iconostasis installed in the 17th century. Here, too, the icons are impressive.

The **Dzhumaya Mosque** dominates the square of the same name. Erected in the 15th century, it's still in use, though many of the almost 50 others built during Ottoman rule have fallen into disrepair. It's worth visiting the smaller **Imaret Mosque** (*ul. Han Krubat*) for its 15th-century lavish interior decoration.

The 19th-century district of Plovdiv is exceptional: a maze of cobbled lanes flanked with fine mansions characterised by brightly coloured façades and overhanging upper floors supported by columns, a style only found here. Though you may be happy simply to take in the vistas, several buildings are worth a special mention and a visit.

Hindlian House (*ul. Artin Gidikov; tel: (032) 628 998; open: Mon–Fri 9am–5pm; admission charge*) was built for wealthy Plovdiv merchant Stefan Hindlian in 1835. The fabric of the house has been thoroughly restored and is furnished with excellent period pieces. **Balabanov House** (*ul. Stoilov 57; tel: (032) 627 082; open: daily 9am–5.30pm; admission charge*) is another merchant's house. It was completely rebuilt from the original plans during the 1980s, and so offers an ideal opportunity to view the style and methods of the architecture as they would have appeared when newly built. The ground floor now contains an art gallery but the upper floors display furniture of the Balabanov family. **Danov House** (*ul. Mitropolit Paisii; tel: (032) 629 405; open: Mon–Fri 9am–noon & 2–5pm; admission charge*) pays homage to Hristo Danov, a famed Bulgarian writer, along with other native authors. Displays include some of the earliest newspapers printed in Bulgaria. For a slightly different experience, head to the **Old Hippocrates Pharmacy** (*ul. Saborna 16; tel: (032) 624 594; open: Mon–Fri 9am–5pm; free admission*). This chemist's shop is unchanged since the late 19th century, its shelves lined with bottles of unguents and potions.

Plovdiv's major museums provide a general overview of the long history of the town. The **Archaeological Museum** (*pl. Saedirenie 1; tel: (032) 633 106; www.archaeologicalmuseumplovdiv.org; open: Tue–Sun 10am–5.30pm; admission charge*) displays items dating from the Neolithic period to the medieval era,

Gateway through Plovdiv's walls

including Thracian, Roman and Byzantine artefacts. The **Ethnographic Museum** (*ul. Dr Chomakov 2; tel: (032) 625 654; open: Tue–Sun 9am–noon & 2–5pm; admission charge*) offers a wide range of objects from furniture and jewellery to traditional handicrafts housed in an exceptional National Revival house built in 1847. There are also good displays of the old trades that kept Plovdiv's economy buoyant – tobacco, wine and handicrafts such as pottery and weaving.

140km (87 miles) southeast of Sofia. Train connections with Burgas, Karlovo, Sofia and Stara Zagora. Bus connections with Karlovo, Sofia and Stara Zagora.

Rilski Manastir (Rila Monastery)

It is ironic that a monastery founded by a hermit should today be Bulgaria's most visited and photographed attraction, but Rila, now a UNESCO World Heritage Site, is perhaps a microcosm of everything that Bulgaria offers to visitors – a spectacular natural setting, exquisite traditional architecture and extravagant religious art.

Founded by Ivan Rilski, also known as John of Rila, in 927, the original Rila complex sat a little way to the northwest but was moved to its present location in 1335, after which it consolidated its position as the most influential monastery in southwestern Bulgaria. It received regular and munificent gifts from the Bulgarian royal family and became an important centre of learning and culture, drawing the finest scholars and artists of each generation. It also negotiated diplomatic accords with other powerful monasteries in Greece and Russia.

During the long years of Ottoman rule, Rila was a strong defender of Bulgarian national identity, keeping the Orthodox faith alive and preserving the nation's culture. Its library has over 16,000 editions, many rare handwritten parchments. The monastery suffered serious damage from insurgents in the early 15th century and a fire in 1833. Much of the complex dates from after 1833, when new donations from across Bulgaria allowed massive investment using the most renowned artisans of their day.

The monastery lies at the heart of the mountains that also bear John of Rila's name. Several precipitous peaks are so close that they seem to peer into the complex over the top of the walls, adding to the wonderful views. The monastery is built within an irregular quadrangle of fortified walls featuring

THE RILA CROSS

The most famous of Rila's artefacts is this wooden cross, also called Raphael's Cross. Created from one piece of wood 80cm by 43cm (31^1/$_2$in × 17in), it is carved with 104 miniature scenes from the Bible featuring more than 650 figures – many no bigger than a grain of rice. Raphael – a monk at the monastery – carved the scenes using a pin as his only tool. As he worked on the piece his eyesight suffered and after 12 years he became blind, so much was he willing to suffer to finish the piece.

The cupolas of Rila Monastery, Bulgaria's top tourist attraction

two entrance gates (the Dupnitza to the west and the Samokov to the east).

At the centre of the interior space sits the magnificent Church of the Nativity, one of the religious masterpieces of the National Revival. Built between 1834 and 1837 in contrasting rows of cream and red tile and stone, it is blanketed in rich murals from the 1840s, depicting Old Testament scenes painted by master Zahari Zograf (though it's certain he had the help of other artists). These are still fairly bright despite the smoke from votive candles. The church also features perhaps the best iconostasis in Bulgaria, begun in 1839. Featuring a riot of intricately carved flowers, animals and human figures framed by columns of vines, it also depicts several biblical scenes. The exterior gallery of the church is also replete with murals whose colours are richer than those of the interior, so it's much easier to take in the detail.

The monastery's museum houses a notable number of artefacts, among them precious icons and other liturgical objects. The museum also proudly displays Rila's charter, signed in 1378 after it moved to its present site. However, pride of place is given to the renowned Rila Cross or Raphael's Cross (*see box opposite*).

The rest of the monastery complex sits around the church and the 25m (82ft) high Hrelyu Tower, the only surviving element of the 1335 building, with a small ornate chapel, the Preobrazhenski or Transfiguration Chapel, on the upper floor.

Designed in high Revival style, the abbot's quarters, cells for over 300

An icon in Rozhen Monastery

monks, the high-ceilinged kitchen, the bakery and the storerooms are all built into the outer walls; these rise to four storeys with a double-arcaded portico all around the complex and wooden balustrades on the upper balconies, which offer panoramic views of the surrounding Rila Mountains. The wooden balconies that punctuate the upper floors are the epitome of Revival style, with ornate wooden carving and gaily painted cornice detail. Four small chapels built in the shape of the Dome of the Cross have also been incorporated into the walls. Each features fine woodcarving and exceptional murals.

There are several other churches in the surrounding hills, all belonging to Rila and reached by footpath. One hour's walk (indicated along a path) from the monastery is the tomb of founder St John or Ivan Rilski in a cave

in the forest (*see walk on pp98–9*). The bones were interred here some 600 years after the saint's death, after being interred in Sofia and Veliko Turnovo. On the way you'll pass St Luke's Hermitage, whose church dates from 1799.

110km (68 miles) south of Sofia; 27km (17 miles) east of Rila village.
Open: daily dawn–dusk. Museum 8.15am–4.15pm. Monastery: free admission. Museum: admission charge. Bus connections with Rila village, from where there are connections to Blagoevgrad. Bus connections from Sofia's Ovcha Kupel bus station.

Rozhenski Manastir (Rozhen Monastery)

Rozhen, officially called the Nativity of the Virgin Mary Monastery, is one of the least visited monasteries. Of the major monastery complexes in Bulgaria it is also the one that best captures the atmosphere of spiritual peace and contemplation. The simplicity of its internal décor is in total contrast to Rila and hints at a more basic life of monastic devotion. Originally founded in 1217, Rozhen was razed by the Turks in the 16th century, and much of what you see today dates from after 1730.

The main church in the monastery, however, dates from 1600 and contains some excellent decoration, including – unusually – some fine, though small, stained-glass windows as well as the more usual murals. The complex refectory is also highly decorated but the rest of the complex features rustic wooden staircases, balconies and balustrades and plain lime-washed walls.

The small church close to the entrance to the monastery is that of Sts Cyril and Methodius and shelters the tomb of Yane Sandanski (1872–1915), a noted Macedonian freedom fighter.

7km (4 1/2 miles) northeast of Melnik. Open: daily dawn–dusk. Free admission but donations welcomed. Bus connections from Melnik and Sandanski to Rozhen village.

Dzhamiya Bairakli Mosque, Samokov

I KNOW THE SCORE!

The small village of Rupite, close to Petrich on the Greek border, was the home of famed Bulgarian clairvoyant Baba Vanga (died 1996), a noted communist. It was her ability to predict the results of football matches that brought her to national attention. Many Bulgarians profited at the bookmakers by following her tips. Because of her influence, Rupite is now the centre of the Bulgarian New Age movement.

Samokov

The first seeds of socialist rule were planted here with the infamous declaration of a commune in 1912, but this experiment in social planning only lasted for two years. Little evidence remains in the town today of that event. Samokov was founded on iron mining and smelting – the town name derives from the Bulgarian word for forge – but was most famed before the commune for its school of icon painting in the 1800s, which produced such luminaries as Zahari Zograf.

The **History Museum** (*open: Mon–Fri 8am–noon & 1–5pm; admission charge*) brings all these diverse strands together with its displays charting the development of iron smelting and old photographs. Other buildings worth visiting are the **Dzhamiya Bairakli Mosque** (*Main square; open: Mon–Fri 8am–noon & 1–5pm; admission charge; tours in English separate charge*), a magnificent National Revival-style edifice constructed in 1840 as the Ottoman grip on power began to falter, the **Convent of Sveta Bogoroditsa**

A rural scene near Shiroka Luka

(*ul. Boris Hadjsotirov 77; open: daily 6am–8pm; free admission*), with its late 17th-century frescoes, and the Church of the Assumption, which possesses an iconostasis of the Samokov School.
60km (37 miles) southeast of Sofia. Bus connections with Borovets, Maliovitsa, Plovdiv and Sofia.

Sandanski

Possibly the birthplace of the legendary Roman slave leader Spartacus, Sandanski sits close to the Greek border. Until 1949, the town was named Melnik but became Sandanski in honour of Macedonian freedom fighter Yane Sandanski. It is known for its thermal springs and balneo-therapeutic clinics, but also offers an alternative base for hiking in the Pirin Mountains.

65km (40 miles) south of Blagoevgrad. Train connections with Blagoevgrad and Sofia. Bus connections with Blagoevgrad, Melnik, Rozhen and Samokov.

Shiroka Luka

An exceptionally picturesque settlement incorporating fine National Revival mansions and three Roman bridges, Shiroka Luka is a protected architectural treasure but is less busy than Koprivshtitsa (*see pp60–62*), allowing you more time to contemplate the architecture. The town is famed for its traditional Bulgarian music and holds one of the most colourful traditional festivals, the *kukeri*, in early March each year, when masked and costumed locals prowl the streets eager to exorcise any lurking demons in order to ensure a good harvest in the coming summer.

15km (9 miles) west of Pamporovo. Bus connection with Smolyan.

Smolyan

Though not a particularly picturesque place in itself, Smolyan, an amalgam of four once independent villages, makes a good base for exploring the central Rodopi Mountains. The town does, however, boast a worthy **Historical Museum** (*Dicho Petrov 3; tel: (0301) 62727; open: Tue–Sun 9am–noon & 1–5pm; admission charge*) tracing a chronological journey through Bulgaria's long past. There's a collection of excellent funerary artefacts from throughout the Thracian period, a huge section on the Bulgarian National Revival and displays of Bulgarian handicrafts, all with useful English captions.

Art lovers will enjoy the **Smolyan Gallery** (*Cultural Complex, Dicho Petrov 7; tel: (0301) 23969; open: Tue–Sun 9am–noon & 1–5pm; admission charge*), which displays around 1,800 paintings by Bulgarian artists dating from the 19th century to the present day.

16km (10 miles) south of Pamporovo. Bus connections with Pamporovo, Plovdiv and Shiroka Luka.
Tourist office: ul. Bulgar 5. Tel: (0301) 62530. Open: Mon–Fri 9am–5.30pm.

The Rodopi Mountains offer walks through unspoilt scenery

Walk: Plovdiv history

With some of the finest examples of Bulgarian National Revival architecture in Bulgaria, the old district of Plovdiv is a picturesque place to wander. This 3km (1³/4-mile) walk will take you from the modern centre to the oldest existing remains of the city, while allowing you to really soak in the street atmosphere. Wear comfortable shoes for the cobbles of the 19th-century district.

Allow 4 hours with visits.

Start at pl. Tsentralen, right in the heart of the modern city, marked by the Trimontium Princess Hotel and a large post office building.

1 Roman forum

Just behind the post office you will find the excavated remains of the Roman forum.

From the square, walk north up ul. Knyaz Aleksander Battenberg, the main shopping street of Plovdiv, with a few international high-street brand names you might recognise.

2 Mosque Square

At the top of Battenberg you'll spot the minaret of the Dzhumaya Mosque, one of the most recognisable landmarks in the city. The small square beside the mosque is filled with artists' stalls. The square is dominated by a column supporting a stylised modern statue of a Roman Caesar, and one look below ground level into the underpass reveals why – this is also the site of the Roman stadium, parts of which now poke out from underneath later buildings.

From the Mosque Square take ul. Saborna (right and behind the mosque from the direction you entered), from where you'll begin to climb into the 19th-century district. Saborna is renowned for its antique shops.

3 Kushta Danov (Danov House)

Danov House sits on the right here in a shady garden. The mansion was owned by celebrated writer and publisher Hristo Danov and its displays showcase the lives of several other Bulgarian authors.

Take the first right beyond Danov House, in front of the Church of the Holy Virgin, then second right (behind the church) along ul. Samokov and right again to ul. Tsar Ivailo to find the Roman Amphitheatre.

4 Roman Amphitheatre

Built in the 2nd century AD and only rediscovered in 1972 following a landslide in the city, today the amphitheatre has been renovated and plays host to open-air performances in the summer.

From the amphitheatre retrace your steps back to Saborna and continue uphill.

5 Gradska Khudozhestvena Galeria
(State Gallery of Fine Arts)

The neoclassical State Gallery of Fine Arts appears on the right. This displays a fine collection of Bulgarian art from the 17th to the 20th centuries. Beyond this is the **Old Hippocrates Pharmacy**. If it isn't open at least you can look through the windows.

Continue up Saborna and you'll find the Church of Sts Konstantin and Elena at the brow of the hill.

6 Church of Sts Konstantin and Elena

This is the oldest church in the city, having been founded in 337 by the Roman Emperor Constantine, though the extravagant murals date from the 1830s when the church was last rebuilt.

It is at this point that the best of Plovdiv reveals itself. Narrow cobbled streets run off left and right, tempting you to leave the main route – each with its own fine buildings worthy of attention. Our route continues uphill along ul. Dr Chumakov.

7 Etnografskiya Muzey (Ethnographical Museum)

On the southeast corner of Chumakov is the Ethnographical Museum, with a series of excellent displays on Bulgarian traditional customs.

Continue past the museum, walking past endearing but unrenovated National Revival mansions, some still family homes, to reach the summit.

8 Nebet Tepe

Atop the hill are the remains of the old Thracian settlement of Eumolpias, with wonderful vistas over the whole city.

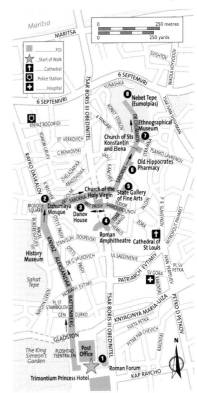

Walk: Kiril Meadows

A host of reasonably signposted footpaths leads out into the hills and mountains surrounding Rila Monastery. However, most involve steep climbs and require sturdy footwear. This walk for the most part follows the road that leads beyond Rila to a mountain basin. The route requires only comfortable footwear rather than specialist hiking boots and the inclines are gradual.

There and back is 13.5km (8¹/₂ miles) – allow 5 hours.

Leave your vehicle in the car park at the monastery and explore the incredible murals in the Church of the Nativity and other parts of the complex before departing through Samokov Gate (the eastern gate), where you'll see the road between cafés and a souvenir shop.

The first section of the walk is almost flat. You'll hear the stream on your right and you'll walk past the Tsarev Hotel. Tightly packed pine trees hug the roadside. You'll walk past a right junction before passing the Zodiac Hotel (also on your right) after 1,300m (1,400yds).

1 At 1.7km (1 mile) the trees recede from the roadside, offering you the first opportunity to view the Rila Mountain peaks before the forest encroaches again.

2 After 3.3km (2 miles) you'll come to a water fountain and some picnic tables on the right. If you didn't bring bottled water with you on the trip, the pure spring water here is perfectly safe to drink.
200m (220yds) beyond the fountain the road swings left and begins to climb more steeply (though it is still a gradual rather than sudden climb).

3 Around this first bend (3.8km/ 2¹/₄ miles from the start of the walk) is a footpath leading to **St Luke's Hermitage** and the tomb of monastery founder Ivan Rilski. Look for the tiny white signpost with the Cyrillic Гробът На Св. Иван Рилски and a painted image of St Ivan with Към гроба above it.

This part of the walk (around 1 hour return) is over rough ground. It leads first to the Hermitage (1843) containing two churches, the Church of St Luke (1799) with a monumental 35-scene Last Judgement mural, and the Church of the Shroud of the Virgin (1805) built by Mihail, a renowned mason from nearby Rila village. The path then carries on to the cave where Rilski lived, having taken a vow to end his days as a hermit. The bones of the saint are now interred here. *Return to the road and continue the gradual climb to your journey's end by turning left.*

4 After 6km (3³/₄ miles) the forest recedes again to reveal an impressive

rocky crest high above you to the left-hand side.

5 At 6.8km (4¹/₄ miles) you reach your destination, a low-lying bowl of grassland and pine forest surrounded on all sides by the Rila Mountains. The views are stupendous and you can picnic under the trees or take advantage of the handful of cafés on site. Further footpaths lead off to higher altitudes, including one that forms part of the E4 Euro-footpath linking the Pyrenees, Alps, Rila and Peloponnese ranges. *From here it's all downhill back to the monastery!*

St Ivan's signpost

Skiing in Bulgaria

Classed as one of Europe's best-value winter sport destinations, Bulgaria has an excellent snow record and offers great choice for the beginner and intermediate skier, though it may not please the 'on-the-edge' thrill seeker searching for the ultimate off-piste experience.

So which area do you choose that meets your needs?

Mount Vitosha

This is just a stone's throw from Sofia, so you could combine a winter visit to the capital with some time on the piste. Thirty kilometres (18^1/$_2$ miles) of runs range from green to black, based around Aleko station, but there are disadvantages. Weekends and holidays are impossibly overcrowded with locals out to enjoy the snow. The infrastructure is also rather old and pistes are not well maintained, but equipment is available for hire.

The Rila Mountains

Borovets is the oldest resort in Bulgaria, established in 1896: a compact centre with three separate satellite settlements (a minibus operates between hotels and the slopes) set in verdant pine forest. The resort has one gondola, two chairlifts and eight surface lifts to cover 50km (31 miles) of pistes, the longest of which is 6km (3^3/$_4$ miles). It's a relatively short transfer from Sofia airport (70km/44 miles).

Malîovitsa is a tiny resort with a couple of hotels and one draglift to

Snow on Mount Vitosha

serve the few runs, but it's cheaper than Borovets and perfectly adequate for an afternoon of fun.

The Pirin Mountains

Bansko has the best snow record of any Bulgarian resort (often enough snow to ski until the end of May) and was a secret the Bulgarians kept to themselves, but that changed with the erection of a state-of-the-art gondola linking the village centre to the slopes (12km/7^1/$_2$ miles away by road). Several new hotels sprang up around the gondola, and Bansko is now an established resort on the skiing market. The main disadvantage is a long transfer from the airport at Sofia (150km/93 miles).

The Rodopi Mountains

Pamporovo is a modern purpose-built resort with a total of 18km (11 miles) of well-maintained pistes (25 runs and 18 lifts, 13 of which are draglifts) aimed at beginners, intermediates and especially families. The ski school here is well established, with multilingual instruction and kids-only lessons. The transfer from Sofia is a long one but most charter flights arrive at Plovdiv only 90km (56 miles) to the north. One disadvantage of Pamporovo is that it is rather spread out and lacking in charm, the opposite of the situation in Borovets.

Snowboarding on the Bansko pistes

Chepelare (two chairlifts only) is a smaller satellite of Pamporovo, but its two main runs are considered to be the best in Bulgaria: the blue run is exceptionally pretty.

Package skiing holidays

To make the most of your skiing budget you may find it cheaper to book a package from home rather than travel independently. Hotels and ski hire shops aren't as geared up for walk-in clients as other European destinations and can charge an extortionate 'rack rate' supplement. You'll also be guaranteed to get decent hire equipment with your package. Look for deals with the major winter snow travel companies.

Ski-run grading

Ski runs in Europe are graded by colour: Greens are the easiest, Blues are slightly more difficult, Reds are more challenging and Blacks are for experts only.

The Black Sea coast

Bulgaria's Black Sea coast is its tourism mecca. It plays host to masses of visitors from Western Europe together with a loyal contingent from Russia. The first tourists arrived in the late 19th century to take the mineral waters found at sources close to Varna, but today it's the fantastic beaches and warm summer weather that are the major draws. Most holidaymakers stay in one of the three huge man-made resorts built since the 1960s, but it's important to break out and enjoy all that the coast has to offer.

Ahtopol

The most southerly point for public transport along the coast, Ahtopol can't yet be described as a tourist resort (though that could change soon). It is, however, a good jumping-off point for Strandjha Nature Park (*see p141*). The town suffered a devastating fire in 1918, so there are scant historical remains, but Bulgarians enjoy the many holiday homes here. Ahtopol has a decent beach, a little distance away from the town centre.
80km (50 miles) southeast of Burgas. Bus connections with Burgas, Kiten and Primorsko.

Albena

Self-styled 'sports capital' of the Black Sea, Albena is set on a spectacular 4km-

(2¹⁄₂ mile) long beach (*see p122*) and offers the most comprehensive range of summer holiday activities in Bulgaria. For this reason it's also one of the most international resorts, with probably the best and most up-to-date infrastructure. Established in 1969 on the site of several mineral springs, the town is named after the heroine of one of Bulgarian playwright Yordan Yovkov's most acclaimed works.

There is no real town, nor are there any historical sights; it is simply an excellent beach resort.
11km (7 miles) south of Balchik. www.albena.bg. Trolleybus transport from hotels to beach. Bus connections with Balchik, Dobrich, Zlatni Pyasutsi and Varna. Parking charge for vehicles.

THE BLACK SEA

The Black Sea borders five other countries: Turkey, Ukraine, Russia, Romania and Georgia. Bulgaria's portion of the 4,000km (2,485-mile) coast is 400km (250 miles).

Balchik

Balchik is a town of steep cobbled lanes flanked by quaint whitewashed and terracotta-tile-roofed cottages set below white chalk cliffs. An early Roman town closer to the shoreline was wiped out by

The Black Sea coast (*see drive pp118–19*)

The Italian-style gardens of Queen Marie's Palace, Balchik

a tidal wave, so 'new' Balchik was rebuilt at a higher elevation in the 7th century AD. In 1913 the region around the town was annexed by Romania. It returned to Bulgarian sovereignty in 1940 but this short period of Romanian rule left the town the legacy of its greatest attraction – the extravagant **Summer Palace of Queen Marie** (*3km/1³/4 miles) west of town on the E87; tel: (0579) 76854; open: daily May–mid-Oct 8am–8pm; mid-Oct–Apr 8.30am–6.30pm; admission charge*).

The English-born queen, consort to King Ferdinand of Romania, wanted a retreat from court life, and this palace, built in the early 1920s, was perfect. Set in 35 hectares (86 acres), the palace is made up of several villas set at different elevations and distances from the sea with a stream, a waterfall and a church all linked by cobbled pathways. An Italianate garden was planted along the seafront with seating areas to enjoy the views. The botanical gardens that grace the palace grounds were developed in

the 1950s and now incorporate around 600 species of plant. The palace and gardens host an annual arts festival in June or July.

In the town itself there are a couple of small but interesting museums. The **History Museum** (*pl. Nezavisimost 1; tel: (0579) 72177; open: Mon–Fri 8am–noon & 1–4.30pm; admission charge*) has some fine ancient Greek and Roman statues, while the **Ethnological Museum** (*ul. Vitosha 3; tel: (0579) 72177; open: Mon–Fri 8am–noon & 1–4.30pm; admission charge*) displays local handicrafts and traditional costumes.

49km (30 miles) north of Varna.
Bus connections with Varna, Dobrich and Albena.

Burgas

Bulgaria's principal port, Burgas (also spelt Bourgas) is a thriving commercial centre. The Thracians and Romans settled here because of the mineral springs, but Burgas really took off in the late 1800s when the railway arrived.

Hemmed in to the coastline by the expansive Burgas Lakes (*see p106*), the suburbs have grown up rather than out, characterised by dour socialist apartment blocks. But the centre of town still has several attractions worth visiting and its tree-lined avenues and several pedestrianised boulevards make it a pleasure to stroll around.

The small **Archaeological Museum** (*ul. Aleko Bogoridi 21; tel: (056) 843 541; open: mid-Jun–mid-Sept Mon–Fri 10am–7pm, Sat 11am–6pm; mid-Sept–mid-Jun Mon–Fri 9am–5pm; admission charge*) displays finds from throughout the town's history, concentrating on the Roman era but including the only wooden Thracian tomb found along the coast.

Brakalov House is home to **Burgas Ethnological Museum** (*ul. Slavyanska 69; tel: (056) 844 423; open: Mon–Fri 9am–6pm, Sat 10am–6pm; admission charge*). It has displays of costumes,

furniture and traditional arts and crafts dating from the late 19th century when the house belonged to Burgas mayor Dimitar Brakalov. The upper floors have some colourful costumes used in traditional Bulgarian folk dances, but all information in the museum is in Cyrillic only.

Burgas Art Gallery (*ul. Mitropolit Simeon 24; www.bourgas.net/art; open: Mon–Fri 9am–noon & 2–6pm; admission charge*), unusually housed in an early 20th-century former synagogue, has an interesting collection of contemporary art by Bulgarian artists, juxtaposed with a small collection of icons.

Between the town and the sea lies Maritime Park, the place where everyone goes to relax or take an evening stroll. With a mixture of formal and informal spaces dotted with sculptures and several cafés, it is also the venue for many activities during Burgas's cultural festivals, the principal

One of the many excursion boats that ply the Black Sea coast

Lake Vaya is home to migrating pelicans in summer

event being the International Folklore Festival in late August.

110km (68 miles) south of Varna. Bus connections with Ahtopol, Kiten, Nesebur, Pomorie, Primorsko, Sozopol, Slunchev Bryag (Sunny Beach) and Varna. Also connections with many towns in central Bulgaria. Tourist office: ul. Lyuben Karavelov 12b. Tel: (056) 813 595.

Burgaski Ezera (Burgas Lakes)

Four large shallow lakes on the landward side of Burgas comprise the largest wetland habitat in Bulgaria. Covering almost 10,000 hectares (25,000 acres), it is frequented by over 300 species of birds, but not all of it is protected and it sits uncomfortably beside the fast-growing port with all its attendant pollution concerns.

You'll find the **Poda Conservation Centre** (*email: poda@bspb.org; open: daily 9am–6pm; admission charge; bus 5, 17 or 18 from Burgas*) at Lake Mandrensko,

around 7km (4 miles) south of Burgas. The centre coordinates all park activities, including guided tours and overnight field trips. From the two viewing platforms at the Poda building you can look out across the lake, the heart of the Poda Protected Area, to spot waders such as ibis or spoonbills, or divers such as cormorants, which seem to be the most prolific species – hundreds of their nests adorn numerous nearby power pylons. A 2.5km (1½-mile) nature walk (*admission charge*) leads deeper into the park, where it's possible to get a little closer to the birds.

Lake Vaya, to the north of Mandrensko, is a seawater habitat and summer home to a vast population of migratory pelicans (best seen Apr–Oct). A boat trip is available (*charge*), but arrangements need to be made through the Poda Conservation Centre.

Buses 17 or 18 to Poda Conservation Centre from Burgas.

Dobrich

Though 36km (22 miles) or so inland from the Black Sea coast, Dobrich is included here because it's a popular and easy day trip from the resorts. During the communist era, Dobrich was renamed Tolbuhin in honour of a Soviet general. Celebrated throughout Bulgaria for its arts and crafts – at its peak it had over 300 workshops – today it is the **Stariyat Dobrich Complex** (*ul. Konstantin Stoilov; open: summer daily 8am–6pm, winter daily 8am–5pm; free admission*) that everyone comes to visit. This tiny quarter of the town – a series of cobbled alleyways – has been transformed into an arts and crafts commune with potters, weavers and printers beavering away in their studios, and it is one of the best places in Bulgaria to buy genuine artisan-crafted souvenirs. You can ponder which purchases you want to make in one of several cafés among the galleries or in the streets off pl. Svoboda. This huge square is typically socialist in its design, surrounded by high apartment blocks and sombre public buildings.

For an insight into the National Revival era visit the pretty **Ethnological Museum** (*ul. 25 Septemvri; open: Mon–Fri 9am–noon & 2–6pm; admission charge*), an 1861 mansion with displays of the 19th-century lifestyles of many regions of Bulgaria.
55km (34 miles) northwest of Albena. Bus connections with Balchik, Varna and Ruse.

Kiten

Set among beachside forests at the southern end of Primorsko Bay, Kiten was abandoned after the fall of the Turks. Not so much a resort as a fragmented collection of buildings, it sits on the marshy mouth of the Karaagach River. This section of coast is pretty much out of the mainstream, excellent for those who want a quieter stay and a more 'Bulgarian' feel. The beach (*see p123*) is certainly the highlight of the town.
55km (34 miles) southeast of Burgas. Bus connections with Primorsko and Ahtopol.

Natsionalen Park Strandzha (Strandjha Nature Park)

See p141.

Nesebur

Probably the one place everybody should visit when they come to the Bulgarian Black Sea, Nesebur (also spelled Nesebâr) is a delightful old town clinging limpet-like to the shell of a narrow rocky isthmus protected by the remnants of once-sturdy ancient Greek and Roman walls. Nesebur is famed for its unique ensemble of Romanesque churches and its fine National Revival mansions, so much so that the town has been designated a World Heritage Site by UNESCO. The downside of it being a must-see attraction is that everyone else wants a piece of the action too – the town is full of day-trippers by late morning. To get the best out of Nesebur arrive

The remains of Roman Nesebur are very much in evidence

early, or stay overnight and enjoy the peace and quiet after the tour buses have departed.

Traces of the early Thracian and Greek settlement of Mesembria now lie below sea level but the Romans built on what is now Nesebur isthmus. As part of the Byzantine Empire from the 5th century, it prospered as a trading port and fortress, but during the latter years of Byzantine rule became a pawn between Constantinople and the Bulgarian Empire, changing hands several times. Each new ruler felt the need to stamp his mark and it was at this time that most of the over 40 churches were erected, each trying to outshine the others. During the years of Turkish rule the fortifications were strengthened but the town declined in importance, only to rise phoenix-like during the Bulgarian National Revival

period. Today it thrives again, on a lifeblood of tourism.

Just on the right after you enter the old town through the impressive remnants of the ancient city walls, the **Archaeological Museum** (*ul. Mesembria 2; tel: (0554) 46019; www.ancient-nessebar.com; email: clio-nes@abv.bg; open: Mon–Fri 9am–7pm, Sat & Sun 9am–1.30pm & 2–6pm; admission charge*) is an excellent place to start your tour. It displays a range of ancient and Byzantine artefacts and a collection of icons salvaged from the town's numerous churches and chapels. Ul. Mesembria forms the arterial route through the town and one can wander along the narrow alleyways that feed from it. The streets are bedecked with traditional lace; almost every house is a souvenir shop.

Nesebur once boasted over 70 churches. Many are now sadly

neglected, but they still form one of the most important collections of Romanesque religious architecture in the world. A selection of icons and murals has been rescued from the ruins, to be displayed in the town Archaeological Museum and the Museum of Icons in Sofia (*see p38*). Only one church, the **Nesebur Orthodox Church**, also known as Sveti Bogoroditsa (*ul. Slavyanska*), is still a place of worship.

The **Pantokrator Church** (*ul. Mesembria*) is the first church you'll see as you travel up into the town from the museum, and it's perhaps most useful as a guide to the 'Nesebur style', with its red and white striped exterior, domes and columns. The

RIDE LIKE THE WIND

Just south of Kiten lies Atliman Bay (Bay of the Horse), so named during the Ottoman era. Legend tells us that a young concubine escaped from the well-guarded harem in the Topkapi Palace in Istanbul. She was eventually recaptured, but the Sultan was so impressed by her guile and bravado that he offered her freedom wherever her horse could ride within the day. She rode north of the city then west along the Black Sea coast to reach the Atliman Bay, and liberty.

interior has now been converted into a commercial gallery. The imposing remains of the **Basilica** (also known as the Metropolitan Church) (*ul. Mesembria*) are the largest in the town. Erected in the 9th century on the site of a 6th-century church, it was the

The harbour at Nesebur

The Church of St John the Baptist dates from the 10th century

seat of the region's bishop, a very rich repository until 1257, when its treasures were looted by the Venetians.

St Stefan's Church (*ul. Ribarska; open: May–Sept Mon–Fri 9am–7pm, Sat & Sun 9am–1pm & 1.30–6pm; closed Oct–Apr; admission charge*) was completed in the 12th century and took over the bishopric after the basilica was ransacked. The three-naved interior exhibits some fine 15th- and 16th-century murals typical of the so-called Nesebur School. The exterior is also decorated with an unusual frill of ceramic and enamel tiles, which represent a development in architectural style at the time. The **Church of St John the Baptist** (*ul. Mitropolitska*), erected in the 10th century, has recently been renovated and also houses a gallery, but should

be visited for the well-preserved 14th-century murals that adorn two of the walls.

A later artistic style can be seen in the remaining frescoes at **St Todor Church** (*ul. Neptun; open: daily 9am–10pm*). Though the **Church of St John Aliturgetos** now lies in ruins after an earthquake in 1913, it probably has the most romantic setting of any church in the town.

Although the churches are without doubt the archaeological highlight of Nesebur, later National Revival buildings now shape the town, offering some of the finest vistas of their kind in eastern Bulgaria. The **Ethnological Museum** (*ul. Mesembria 34; open: daily 10am–1pm & 2–6pm; admission charge*) is a case in point. Set in a typical National Revival house, it displays a range of national and folk costumes and traditional fabrics.

35km (22 miles) northeast of Burgas. Bus connections with Burgas, Varna and Slunchev Bryag. Don't park just outside the town walls, or you will be towed away. Park your car in the car park just before the isthmus and walk the 300m (330yds) into the old town.

Nos Kaliakra (Cape Kaliakra)

Cape Kaliakra is the northern limit of the tourist infrastructure on the Black Sea coast. Beyond this pointed spur projecting southward into the sea you will find only tiny villages until the Romanian border.

Kaliakra Nature Reserve (*see p138*), an important protected area for seabirds, seals and dolphins, covers much of the cape.

70km (44 miles) northeast of Varna.

Bus connections with Balgarevo 8km (5 miles) from the tip.

Pomorie

Destroyed by fire in 1906, Pomorie is a shadow of its former self. The shallow bay to the north of town with its lagoon and natural sand spit is one of the best locations on the coast for wind- and kite-surfing. The town beach isn't bad but the tourism infrastructure lags behind other resorts on this part of the coast.

20km (12½ miles) northeast of Burgas. Bus connections with Burgas, Nesebur and Slunchev Bryag.

Primorsko

Primorsko is a lower-key resort than those north of Burgas, seeing more Bulgarian visitors than foreign tourists. The curved sheltered beach is an

The Black Sea coast

The coastline at Cape Kaliakra

Sozopol's pretty waterfront has been busy with shipping since ancient times

attraction but there's little else to see here. *50km (31 miles) southeast of Burgas. Buses to Burgas and Kiten.*

Priroden Rezervat Ropotamo (Ropotamo Nature Reserve)

See p139.

Slunchev Bryag (Sunny Beach)

The largest purpose-built resort on the Black Sea coast, the site of Sunny Beach, as it's known in English, was chosen because of its excellent strand (*see p122*). Over 100 hotels offer just about everything families need for a perfect package holiday and many are set in ample grounds with pools and sports facilities. Its only role is as a package destination – so much so that the whole place pretty much closes down between October and April. There's little genuine Bulgarian charm here. Most holidaymakers try to find that by taking day trips to nearby Nesebur (it's a pleasant walk from one to the other along the beach). *5km (3 miles) north of Nesebur. Bus connections with Burgas, Nesebur, Pomorie and Varna.*

Sozopol

Rivalling Nesebur in its character (though not in architectural importance), old Sozopol is a characterful cluster of National Revival houses set on narrow cobbled streets. It's home to a thriving artistic community and its good town beaches and lively nightlife make it the best all-round resort on the Black Sea.

It was first inhabited by the Thracians from 4000 BC and they were joined by the Greeks in around 600 BC; the combined populations thrived on trade until the town, then named Apollonia, was razed by Roman forces in 72 BC. Though it revived later under Roman occupation, it fell into decline following the fall of the Empire and spent much of the last millennium being used as a simple fishing village.

Sozopol was abandoned following the Russo-Turkish War (1878), when the population feared Turkish reprisals. It was many decades before it was resettled.

There are few specific attractions here. The **Archaeological Museum** (*ul. Han Krum 2; tel: (0550) 22267; open: summer daily 8am–6pm; winter Mon–Fri 8am–6pm; admission charge*) has some finds discovered by marine biologists just offshore, and the **Art Gallery** (*ul. Kiril & Metodii 70; open: Mon–Sat 10am–7.30pm; admission charge*) has a collection of seascapes. Occupying a historic house, the **Ethnographic Museum** (*ul. Kiril & Metodii 34; tel: (0550) 22748; open: Mon–Fri 8am–6pm; admission charge*) contains old photos of the town plus other memorabilia. Providing less formal attractions, many of Sozopol's buildings now house bars, cafés and

Tourism has replaced fishing as Sozopol's main source of income

shops and it's the perfect place for a stroll on a warm summer evening.

Just offshore from Sozopol is **St John's Island**, now an uninhabited nature reserve covering over 650 hectares (1,600 acres). You can visit by boat from the Kraybrezhna quay (*admission charge*) and birdwatch or explore the remains of a ruined Byzantine monastery.
30km (18½ miles) southeast of Burgas. Bus connections with Burgas, Ahtopol, Primorski and Kiten.

Sveti Konstantin

Founded just after World War II on a source of mineral springs, the resort of Sveti Konstantin was originally called Druzhba, meaning Friendship, but today takes its name from the tiny church of Sveti Konstantin and Sveti Elena, built in the 18th century in the centre of town. A number of hotel spa complexes sit among pine forests and here you can enjoy massages and other forms of treatment (*see pp164–5*). There's also a reasonable beach.
10km (6 miles) northeast of Varna. Bus connections with Varna; also Varna to Zlatni Pyasutsi buses will stop at Sveti Konstantin.

Varna

Varna, Bulgaria's third-largest city, is the major conurbation of the Black Sea coast. Its position on the mouth of the Varnensko estuary, backed by the rolling hills of the Frangensko Plateau, has been coveted as far back as 4000 BC, when the Thracians founded the first

ROMAN BATHS

Bath complexes were an integral part of the social life of the Roman city at a time when citizens (as opposed to slaves) had lots of free time to fill. No expense was spared in the sophistication of the plumbing, the quality of the building or the interior décor. Along with steam and massage rooms, the *thermae* consisted of a series of rooms: the hot water rooms (*caldarium*), tepid water rooms (*tepidarium*) and cold rooms (*frigidarium*). To gain the most benefit one started with a dip in the *frigidarium*, working through the temperature ranges to the *caldarium*.

settlement here. However, it was the Romans who really put Varna (then called Odessos) on the map.

In the late 1800s Varna enjoyed another economic rejuvenation when

Old wooden houses in a Sozopol street

the railway linked it with Ruse on the Danube, completing an important industrial transport conduit. The nearby mineral spas and beaches also attracted holidaymakers from the earliest era of tourism. Today it's a cultural highlight of the region, with a multitude of summer festivals and galleries galore.

The **Varna Archaeological Museum** (*ul. Maria Luisa 41; tel: (052) 681 011; open: summer Tue–Sun 10am–5pm; winter Tue–Sat 10am–5pm; admission charge*) is the largest museum in Bulgaria, offering the best display of ancient artefacts in the country. It's a mammoth collection that needs some time to take in fully. The collections are set out chronologically and have English captions, which makes everything easy to follow. Make a point of viewing objects discovered at the Varna Thracian Necropolis, as the complex (west of town) is now closed to the public. The finds, dating from 4000 BC, include gold jewellery of amazing workmanship. The Roman galleries are also impressive, despite some finds having been spirited away to Sofia.

The town's **Ethnological Museum** (*ul. Panagyurishte 22; tel: (052) 650 588; open: daily 10am–5pm in summer; Tue–Sat 10am–5pm in winter; admission charge*) brings more recent Bulgarian social history to life. Housed in a National Revival mansion of *c.* 1860, it features furniture from the period. There are displays on winemaking, on the once-thriving

Varna Archaeological Museum

fishing industry and on recent but now lost agricultural customs.

However, not all of Varna's archaeological jewels lie hidden in shady rooms. The largest church in the town is the beautiful **Cathedral of the Assumption** (*pl. Mitropolitska Simeon; open: daily 6am–10pm*). Completed in 1886 in archetypal Orthodox style, it is decorated with 20th-century frescoes. The much fêted 2nd-century AD **Roman Spa** (*ul. San Stefano; tel: (052) 600 059; open: summer Tue–Sun 10am–5pm; winter Tue–Sat 10am–5pm; admission charge*) is a little disappointing. Of the third-largest Roman baths complex so far identified in Europe, and certainly the most extensive in Bulgaria, only a fraction remains in reasonable condition. Far more impressive is the

The Sea Gardens

St Anastasios Orthodox Church (*ul. Graf Ignatiev*), built on top of the spa at its eastern corner in 1602, though the interior was totally renovated after the departure of the Ottomans. The interior is a riot of gilt with a fine iconostasis and some worthy modern icons.

After the cultural delights, do what the locals do and head for the **Sea Gardens**. Almost 100 hectares (250 acres) of woods and gardens run for 7km (4¹/₄ miles) along the shoreline of the Black Sea, and in summer there's always something happening – concerts, festivals and street entertainers – plus the draw of the adjacent beach. The Sea Gardens have their own collection of attractions: **Zoopark** (*tel: (052) 302 528; open: daily 8am–6pm; admission charge*) for animals, **Terrarium Varna** (*tel: (052) 302 571; open: daily 9am–9pm; admission charge*) for spiders and such, the **Aquarium** (*tel: (052) 632 066; open: Tue–Sun 9am–5pm; admission charge*) and the **Dolphinarium** (*shows Tue–Sun 10.30am, noon & 3.30pm summer only;*

admission charge). You'll also find the largest **Naval Museum** (*tel: (052) 632 018; open: summer daily 10.30am–6pm; winter Mon–Fri 8.30am–5pm; admission charge*) in Bulgaria, with a motley collection of old and tired vessels.
110km (68 miles) north of Burgas. Varna Airport is the main point of entry for domestic scheduled and international charter flights. Buses to points across Bulgaria; local connections with Burgas, Dobrich, Nesebur and Slunchev Bryag.

Zlatni Pyasutsi (Golden Sands)

Called Golden Sands in English, this modern purpose-built resort (also spelt Zlatni Pyasâtsi) is set on one of the best beaches along the coast (*see pp122–3*). Taking the majority of its holidaymakers from abroad, it has little Bulgarian character but good facilities for a beach-based holiday.

Close by is **Aladzha Manastir** (Aladzha Monastery) (*open: May–Oct daily 9am–6pm; Nov–Apr daily 9am–4pm; admission charge*), a complex of caves carved out of the rocky cliffs backing the resort during the early years of Ottoman occupation. The caverns (signposted 'Catacombs') lie up to 40m (130ft) above ground level and are reached by a series of ladders and stairways; they are decorated with interesting, though faded, murals. The small museum on site explains how the caves were carved.
20km (12½ miles) north of Varna. Bus connections with Varna.

Varna's Cathedral of the Assumption

Drive: The southern Black Sea coast

This drive allows you to break out of Sunny Beach to discover some of the natural and historic sites of the southern coast. It's a full day of activities, but you are never far from refreshment to keep your energy levels high, and you can always cool down at one of the many beaches.

Distance: 180km (112 miles); allow 8 hours. See map on p103.

Leave the resort on the main E87/A9 road. Just beyond the southernmost hotels of the resort there is a left turn to Nesebur which leads through the modern part of town to the isthmus, where you'll see the old part of town. Park in the large car park on the right just before the causeway that links the isthmus to the mainland.

1 Nesebur

This is one of the cultural highlights of the entire country and a UNESCO World Heritage Site. Stroll along the cobbled lanes to enjoy the pretty 19th-century mansions and explore the numerous Romanesque churches. Nesebur is also a great place to buy your holiday souvenirs.

After Nesebur, head south on the coast road (E87/A9) in the direction of Burgas. After 22km (13½ miles) it's possible to take a left turn to the resort of Pomorie, with its excellent windsurfing, but this drive takes you on to the more impressive highlights. Continue along the main E87/A9 road.

2 Burgas Lakes

Ten kilometres (6 miles) south of Pomorie you'll pass between the two northerly Burgas Lakes, a rich environment for birdlife. Keep a watch out for huge flocks of pelicans, gulls and wading birds such as spoonbills.

A windmill in Nesebur

17km (10½ miles) south of Pomorie on the main E87/A9 you'll arrive in the centre of Burgas.

3 Burgas

Burgas is a large town but has some pleasant pedestrianised streets to facilitate exploration. Visit the Archaeological and Ethnological Museums before heading to the shade of Maritime Park.

Pick up the E87/A9 south of the town (signposted Sozopol) to continue your journey. 7km (4½ miles) out of town look out for a small building on the left marked PODA.

4 Burgas Lakes Visitor Centre

This is the visitor centre for the Burgas Lakes complex. There's a small display on the birdlife you can see on the lakes (not all species inhabit the lakes all year round), but the highlight is the view across the marshes of the southern lakes from its observation platforms. Binoculars are supplied to help you get a clearer view.

Continue southeast another 20km (12½ miles) to Sozopol.

5 Sozopol

Perhaps the most 'rounded' of the Black Sea resorts, Sozopol has a little bit of everything. This is the perfect place to have lunch or a cooling drink surrounded by National Revival architecture in the old town or by the pretty town beach.

From Sozopol it's only 10km (6 miles) south to the Ropotamo Nature Reserve.

Traditional architecture in Burgas

6 Ropotamo Nature Reserve

This reserve protects vast natural marshes that form an important environment for rare fauna and flora, including desert orchids. The sand dunes here are the most extensive in Bulgaria. Enjoy a boat trip or a walk around the public area of the park and then head just to the north to the tiny resort of Dyuni. You can spend some time on the beach here while you decide whether to extend your journey south to the smaller resorts of Kiten and Ahtopol, and finally to the remote Strandjha Nature Park hugging the border with Turkey (an extra 100km/ 62 miles return), or head north back to Sunny Beach.

Walk: Central Varna

Varna makes the perfect excursion destination: lots to see, and pleasant, mostly pedestrian-only streets to link the various attractions. The Sea Gardens are a great place to break your trip, especially if you have children, and there are lots of cafés to stop at for an excellent fortifying Bulgarian coffee.

This walk will take about 4 hours (longer if you linger in the park or at the beach).

1 Arkheologicheski Muzey (Archaeological Museum)

Start at the neoclassical Archaeological Museum, the largest in the country, with a comprehensive range of ancient artefacts.

From the museum walk along bul. Maria-Luiza; after 400m (440yds) you'll reach pl. Metropolit Simeon.

2 Cathedral of the Assumption

On your right, the domes and arches of the Cathedral of the Assumption come into view. This is arguably Bulgaria's finest 19th-century urban church outside Sofia and is an emblem of the town. Some interesting 20th-century icons grace the interior. The pretty gardens around the church square are one of the best places to buy traditional lace souvenirs. The lady stallholders sit making new pieces while they display their wares.

From the church, take the underpass under four-lane bul. Maria-Luiza to reach the top of pedestrian street ul.

Preslav. Walk down Preslav for around 200m (220yds) to pl. Nezavisimost.

3 Ploshtad Nezavisimost (Independence Square)

This pleasant, leafy square is lined with shady cafés. Look out for the cupola of Varna Opera House on your right as you enter the square.

Continue down ul. Preslav. Another major pedestrian thoroughfare, bul. Knyaz Boris I, heads off left (with some good modern shopping opportunities), but carry on until you find ul. Panagyurishte on the right (the first main street after Knyaz Boris I). At the next junction, you will see the Ethnological Museum.

4 Etnografski Muzey (Ethnological Museum)

This National Revival mansion is furnished with period pieces. It presents a perfect opportunity to step back into one of Bulgaria's heydays.

Retrace your steps to ul. Preslav

and take a right to a small square. Straight across the square is ul. San Stefano. Take this and the first junction left, ul. Khan Krum, to find the entrance to the Roman Spa.

5 Rimskite Termi (Roman Spa)

This half-excavated vaulted complex gives an impression of just what delights remain under the modern city and is one of the largest of its kind in Europe.

6 Church of St Anastasios

Above the baths is the Church of St Anastasios (*ul. Graf Ignatiev*), with its ultra-ornate Orthodox interior. *From the church walk left down ul.*

Graf Ignatiev, then cross busy ul. Primorski to enter the Sea Gardens.

7 Sea Gardens

Once you've explored the park or spent some time on Varna's adjacent town beach, take the main park entrance out back into the town. This pedestrianised area, forming a bridge over ul. Primorski, leads into an open square with the modern Festival Hall on your left and bul. Slivnitsa straight ahead.

Walk up Slivnitsa until you reach the end of the road, then turn left. The road will become bul. Maria-Luiza, bringing you back to the Archaeological Museum.

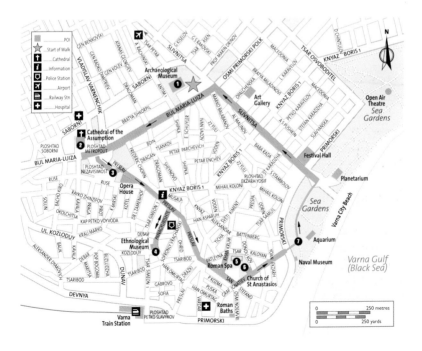

Black Sea beaches

The Black Sea is famed for its beaches, but it isn't just one long stretch of sand. Here's some information to help you make your choice.

Major resorts

The 'big three' resorts anchor tourism on the Black Sea, with plenty of bars and restaurants. You'll also have lots of company, especially in July and August.

Albena is the most upmarket resort. Purpose-built on 4km (2$\frac{1}{2}$ miles) of fine golden sand, the beach is exceptionally good for children because it has a wide stretch of coastal shallows so they can paddle and swim in relative safety. There are also plenty of watersports and around 50 hotels. Much of the resort is traffic-free and there's a long seafront promenade lined with restaurants, bars and cafés.

Slunchev Bryag (Sunny Beach) has probably the longest beach along the coast, a magnificent 8km (5 miles) of sand over 100m (110yds) wide: the perfect location for a holiday resort. There are excellent facilities for young children. Most of the 100 or so hotels crowd the southern half of the beach and walking a couple of kilometres (1$\frac{1}{4}$ miles) north gives you more space.

The Big Wheel is a major draw for families at Golden Sands

Zlatni Pyasutsi (Golden Sands) is now the largest resort along the coast and its beach is beautiful, though at 3.7km (2^1/4 miles) long it's only half the length of Sunny Beach and caters to about the same number of hotels.

Sunny Beach view

Smaller resorts

The travel brochures also feature several other less manufactured and commercialised resorts.

Pomorie's town beach is broken by a series of groynes (wooden barriers) designed to stop the sand from being eroded by the sea. It is sandy but narrow and it does get very busy.

Sozopol has a good sand beach in the town but it's rather small, so you'll need to arrive early to get a decent sunbed.

Sveti Konstantin's beach is not one long continuous stretch of sand but rather smaller coves broken by rocky outcrops.

Quieter resorts

Those who want less crowded beaches and perhaps a more genuinely Bulgarian atmosphere have several options.

Ahtopol is a relaxed resort (for the time being at least – a huge yacht marina is planned) in the south, set on a cape flanked by two long sandy beaches. The northern one is renowned throughout Eastern Europe

as a nudist beach. About 5km (3 miles) south of the town is the outlet of the Veleka River, barred by a sandy spit offering seawater swimming to the east and cooler freshwater swimming in the river to the west.

Kiten, also in the south, sits close to the beautiful horseshoe-shaped Atliman Beach, with its exceptional azure blue shallows.

Two smaller resorts between Varna and Burgas are **Byala** and **Obzor**. If you want a low-key, cosy resort with a few eateries combined with a good beach, then these are ideal.

For the ultimate in 'get away from it all' Black Sea coast beaches, you'll need to head south into **Strandjha Nature Park** (*see p141*). This protected corner of Bulgaria hugs the Turkish border. There is little in the way of tourist infrastructure but you'll definitely be rewarded by totally unspoilt strands. **Silistar Beach** is the best. Blessed with golden sand and shallow azure waters, it's still relatively unknown – you'll just have to hurry before the secret gets out!

Northern Bulgaria

Visitors tend to forsake the north for the more obvious delights south and east of Sofia, leaving much of the area north of the Stara Planina Mountains remarkably free of foreign tourists. But Bulgaria's least visited region has several worthy attractions, including exceptional fortifications, unspoilt natural landscapes, and the most renowned rock tomb in the country.

Belogradchik

Set dramatically among immense red rock formations, Belogradchik derives its name from the Bulgarian *beliya gradezh*, the white building, after the strong granite fortress that dominates the town.

Founded by the Romans and expanded by the Byzantines, the **citadel** (*open: daily Jun–Sept 9am–8pm, Oct–May 9am–5pm; admission charge*) was occupied throughout Bulgaria's history until the 18th century because it

protected the northern route towards what is now Romania. In 1850 a localised peasant uprising was brutally put down by the Ottomans. The last few rebels were slaughtered in the citadel. Much of what you see today is 17th-century Ottoman. Magnificent buttress walls and fine tower entrance portals – this is how a castle should look.

The old quarter of the town below is gradually being renovated under the Beautiful Bulgaria Project (*see p55*) but it is still work in progress. Head to the **History Museum** (*pl. 1850 Leto; open: Mon–Fri 9am–noon & 2–5pm; admission charge*) for assorted artefacts found at the fortress and geological information about the Belogradchik rocks.
52km (32 miles) south of Vidin. Bus connections with Vidin and Montana.

Cherepishki Manastir (Cherepish Monastery)

Nestling on the banks of the Iskur River at the foot of the high curtain walls of the river valley, Cherepish is one of the smallest and most peaceful monasteries in Bulgaria. The retreat has gruesome antecedents, founded after a bloody 14th-century battle won by Tsar Ivan Shishman. It is said that he ordered the skulls of the dead to be piled high and ordained that a monastery should be founded on that very spot. Cherepish is derived from *cherep*, the Bulgarian word for skull. The monastery was the subject of a number of raids by Ottoman forces

Cherepish Monastery

and was the leading Haidouk refuge (*see pp78–9*) in the northwest.

The monastery has few important religious relics, though the church has a set of three works by Patriarch Evtimii and written documents dating from the 15th century. It is much more the atmosphere and setting here that is the attraction. Just outside the walls the monastery has built three blocks of simple rooms and this is one of the best places in Bulgaria to enjoy a few days of peace and contemplation.
70km (43 miles) north of Sofia. Open: 24 hours. Free admission. Buses from Sofia to Vratsa will stop on the main road 1km (²/₃ mile) from the monastery entrance.

Cherven

Set on the very southern tip of one of the spurs of the Rusenski Lom National Park, Cherven is a tiny settlement now opening up to tourism because of the medieval citadel overlooking the valley.

Ivanovo Rock Monastery

One of the best preserved of its type in the Balkans and used as a template for restorations taking place in Veliko Turnovo (*see pp70–75*), the citadel – an important trading and defensive town during the 13th and 14th centuries – has the remains of the city walls, streets, churches and inner fortifications available for exploration. *40km (25 miles) south of Ruse. Bus connections with Ruse.*

Ezero Sreburna (Lake Sreburna)
See pp140–41.

Ivanovskiyat Skalen Manastir (Ivanovo Rock Monastery)
Bulgaria's most famous cave monastery, Ivanovo (officially the St Archangel Michael Monastery), was hewn out of the cliffs above the Rusenski River during the 1400s with funds supplied directly from the Bulgarian royal

family. This royal patronage allowed the best artisans to be employed in the decoration of the interior and on the murals by the Turnovo School in the Church of St Bogoroditsa (the Holy Virgin), which constitute the major visitor attraction and are considered the best in the Balkans, particularly the evocative *Last Supper*. The church is on the UNESCO World Heritage Site list but is in a poor state of repair, with several sections of the roof looking rather fragile.
20km (12½ miles) south of Ruse. Open: Wed–Sun 9am–noon & 2–5pm. Admission charge. Bus connections from Ivanovo village, 4km (2½ miles) from the site, to Ruse.

Ruse
Set on Bulgaria's northeastern border on the banks of the Danube, Ruse was first settled by the Romans, but it wasn't important again to Bulgarians until the railway arrived. When the Ruse to Varna line opened in 1866, completing the Black Sea–Danube conduit, it vastly increased trade and boosted the economy of the whole country, but the money and commerce were concentrated here.

When the Ottomans left Bulgaria, Ruse was the country's most prosperous city and its architecture is influenced by the styles fashionable in the Austro-Hungarian Empire to the north, with which it mainly traded. Ploshtad Svoboda, at the heart of the town, demonstrates this well and is perhaps

THE FRIENDSHIP BRIDGE

Despite Bulgaria's long northern river border, Ruse is the only town to have a fixed link with Romania; the rest have ferry connections. The Friendship Bridge was begun in 1949 and opened in 1954. A monumental engineering project, it is 3km (1^3/$_4$ miles) long and stands 30m (100ft) above the river. The bridge was not designed to take pedestrian traffic, so you'll need to ride in a vehicle to travel across it.

the finest square in Bulgaria, flanked by neoclassical façades – look particularly for **Dohodnoto Zdanie** (the Profitable Building), erected in 1902. The Monument to Freedom erected in 1908 sits at its heart, surrounded by a small park where locals while away the warm summer evenings.

The Museum of Urban Life (*ul. Tsar Ferdinand 39; tel: (082) 820 997; open: Mon–Fri 9am–noon & 2–5pm; admission charge*) is a late 19th-century house fully furnished in a style typical of the time with a good collection of contemporary porcelain and glass.

Of course Ruse had its own 19th-century freedom fighters. The **family home of Zahari Stoyanov** now houses a **museum** (*bul. Pridunavski 14; tel: (082) 820 996; open: Mon–Fri 9am–noon & 2–5pm; admission charge*) paying homage to the man, who was also a politician and writer. In the east of the city, the gardens of Revivalists' Park surround the Pantheon of the National Revival, which commemorates the revolutionary leaders and local people who lost their lives during the Bulgarian liberation.

The oldest church in the city is the **Sveta Troitsa** (*pl. Sveta Troitsa; open: daily 7am–6pm; free admission*). Designed in Russian style, it has some fine 16th-century murals. The (Catholic) Church of St Paul the Crucified (1890) has the country's earliest organ, installed in 1907.

Though the Danube is a mighty river it plays little part in the daily lives of the people. A badly tended waterfront park is spoilt by the nearby railway line. There's only one small boat offering river cruises and the busy waterway is crowded with industrial barges. However, the original Ruse station, the oldest in Bulgaria, has now been transformed into a small **railway museum** (*ul. Bratya-Obretenov 5; tel: (082) 803 516; open: Mon–Fri 8am–noon & 2–5pm; admission charge*) relating to rail and river transport. You can also find remnants of the original 1st-century AD Roman fortress **Saxaginta Prista** by the waterside (*ul. Tsar Kaloyan 2; tel: (082) 825 004; open: Mon–Fri 9am–noon & 1–5pm; admission charge*), including the river

The fine neoclassical façade of Dohodnoto Zdanie in Ruse

Northern Bulgaria

docks, towers and sleeping quarters of the legionaries.

Priroden Park Rusenski Lom (Rusenski Lom Nature Park)

See pp139–40.

Silistra

Silistra sits at the point on the Danube where the river leaves Bulgarian soil, cutting north into Romania. It's been settled since Roman times, and adopted Christianity early, becoming an important episcopal centre during the first millennium. The fortresses in the hills above also bear witness to its role as a guardian of borders throughout the last 1,800 years. Silistra was the focal point of many minor military actions between Russians and Turks during the 19th century – the author Tolstoy took part in a siege of the town in 1854. From 1913 until 1940 this part of the country was appropriated by Romania. The town is famed for its apricot brandy, and apricot orchards blanket the surrounding valleys.

The large 19th-century Medzhitabiya Turkish fortress is the most formidable building in town but it's closed to the public. Much smaller, but equally impressive, is the 4th-century AD Roman tomb discovered in 1942, which is decorated with colourful murals. Other elements of the Roman settlement dot the town. The **Archaeological Museum** (*G. S. Rakovski; tel: (086) 823 894; open: Tue–Sun 8am–noon & 2–6pm; admission charge*) displays finds from both locations, together with a rare Thracian chariot.

120km (75 miles) east of Ruse.
Bus connections with Dobrich, Ruse, Shumen and Varna.

Vidin

Set in the northernmost corner of Bulgaria on the banks of the Danube looking across into Romania, Vidin has been gentrified under the Beautiful Bulgaria Project (*see p55*); its once-fine houses have been brought back to life after decades of neglect. In the 14th century the city and its environs declared independence from the Second Empire. It fell into Ottoman hands but a local tribal lord staged a rebellion in the early 19th century, seeking assistance from Napoleon. Even today its people are considered a little aloof from the rest of the Bulgarian population.

Set on one of the Danube's easier crossing sites, it was settled by the Romans, who built a fort to protect the northern border. During the Second Bulgarian Empire it resumed this role and **Baba Vida Fortress** (*ul. Baba Vida; tel: (094) 601 705; open: Mon–Fri 8.30am–5pm, Sat & Sun 10am–5pm;*

LOCKED OUT

Two Russian generals stole the key to the fortress at Silistra in 1810 during one of the Russian army's regular skirmishes with the Turks. It was taken to St Petersburg, where it remained until 1958 before being ceremonially handed back into the safe hands of Silistra town officials.

admission charge), now dominating the town, was built. One of the most splendid and complete in the Balkans, the fortress was built at various stages from the 10th to the 14th centuries, though the Turks consolidated the walls in the 17th century. Because of its rebellion and semi-independence, Vidin was spared the fighting during the Russo-Turkish War and the fort was undamaged. The Austro-Hungarian Habsburgs usurped it for a short period in the 19th century.

Back in town, the **Archaeological Museum** (*ul. Targovska; open: Tue–Sat 9am–noon & 1.30–5.30pm; admission charge*) has a comprehensive collection of Neolithic finds from the local region and Roman artefacts from Vidin itself and from the site of Ratiaria 25km (15¹/₂ miles) to the south.
100km (62 miles) northwest of Montana. Bus connections with Belogradchik, Montana and Pleven.

Vratsa

Ignore the grey industrial suburbs that surround the centre of Vratsa. In the heart of the town you'll find tree-lined boulevards, pedestrianised streets with shops and cafés and a large central square, perfect for a stroll.

The town is often used as a base for hiking and climbing in the Vrachanska Balkan National Park, just to the west of town, and there are several monasteries in close proximity.

Revered Bulgarian freedom fighter Hristo Botev (*see p79*) was killed close

The Baba Vida Fortress in Vidin

by during the uprising, and the town makes the most of the connection. The main square is named after him and sports a monument to him. The **Historical Museum** (*pl. Hristo Botev; tel: (092) 620 220; open: Tue–Sun 9am–noon & 3–7pm; admission charge, ticket also valid for Ethnological Museum Complex*) has a section concerning Botev but is more noteworthy for its range of displays that include some good Thracian artefacts and items produced by Vratsa goldsmiths, an important industry during the 19th century.

Vratsa's **Ethnological Museum Complex** (*ul. General Leonov; tel: (092) 620 209; open: Tue–Sun 9am–noon & 2–5pm; admission charge, ticket also valid for Historical Museum*) comprises several National Revival buildings whose highlights include a good collection of national costumes. Kemara, the old craftsmen's quarter in the south of the town, houses artisans.
116km (72 miles) north of Sofia. Train and bus connections with Sofia and Vidin.

Walk: Central Ruse

The centre of Ruse reveals grand neoclassical architecture of a kind not usually found in Bulgaria outside the capital.

This 3km (1³/₄-mile) walk, taking about 3 hours, starts at and is centred on the main square in the town, pl. Svoboda or Freedom Square.

1 Ploshtad Svoboda

Arguably the finest plaza in Bulgaria, this is the hub of the city. The formal gardens at its centre provide an ideal meeting place, under the shadow of the Monument to Freedom, erected in

1908. The most splendid building on the square is the **Dohodnoto Zdanie** (the Profitable Building) of 1902.
Leave pl. Svoboda by bul. Aleksandrovska, keeping the Law Courts building to your right, until you reach pl. Battenberg.

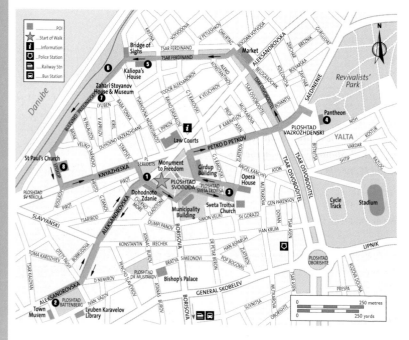

2 Ploshtad Battenberg

Once the main square of the city, Battenberg also displays some fine late 19th- and early 20th-century façades. Look particularly for the **Town Museum** and the **Lyuben Karavelov Library**.
Return to pl. Svoboda and leave it by pl. Sveta Troitsa (with the Municipality Building on your right).

3 Ploshtad Sveta Troitsa

Pl. Sveta Troitsa has two important buildings: the **Sveta Troitsa Church** (the oldest in Ruse, completed in 1632) and the **Ruse Opera House**.
Return to pl. Svoboda and leave by ul. Petko Petkov (to the left of the Danube Plaza Hotel). Cross busy bul. Tsar Osvoboditel to reach Revivalists' Park.

4 Revivalists' Park

This was once the city cemetery, where many heroes of the struggle for freedom were buried. In 1978 a small **Pantheon** was built here and the bones of many of the dead re-interred in the building.
Return to bul. Tsar Osvoboditel and turn right. Follow the highway as it becomes bul. Tsar Ferdinand. The monument to Stefan Karadzha is on the right.

5 Kushtata na Kaliopa (Kaliopa's House)

Further down on the left just before the road meets the river is Kaliopa's House, home to the Museum of Urban Life.
Turn left where bul. Tsar Ferdinand meets bul. Pridunavski.

6 The Danube

The famous river wends its way eastward just across the railway line. A park allows access to the riverbank.

7 Kushtata-muzey Zahari Stoyanov (Zahari Stoyanov House & Museum)

On the landward side of bul. Pridunavski you'll find the house and museum of Zahari Stoyanov, a prominent revolutionary and politician.
Continue along bul. Pridunavski.

8 St Paul's Church

Further along this boulevard, this Catholic church is the repository of Bulgaria's first church organ.
Keep going until you reach ul. Knyazheska. Turn left here and it leads back to pl. Svoboda.

Architecture in the Austro-Hungarian style dating from Ruse's heyday

The Danube

The River Danube is one of Europe's great waterways. The very mention of its name conjures up images of genteel cruises past vine-draped, sun-drenched hills and the occasional *Schloss* or two accompanied by the dulcet tones of Johann Strauss's stirring waltz. Unfortunately, by the time the river gets to Bulgaria, it's a slightly different story. If the water was ever blue, it certainly isn't today! The detritus of five countries floats past here every day.

Throughout the communist era, the river was viewed principally as a transport route, and urban river banks were used to facilitate deliveries to and from Russia's vast Black Sea coast. The idea that the Danube could be used for pleasure or leisure was anathema to the socialist authorities and they remained staunchly indifferent to its important role as a provider of natural habitat.

Some progress was made in 1983 with the creation of the Sreburna Nature Reserve (*see pp140–41*), protecting the 8,000 hectares (20,000 acres) of shallow lake with an outlet into the Danube, and recognised by UNESCO as a World Heritage Site for its role as a migratory haven for birds.

Unfortunately Bulgaria couldn't isolate its section of the Danube from the dangers that other countries posed, and in March 1988 a chemical spillage at Giurgiu in Romania caused an environmental disaster for the lower Danube that the scientists estimated would take 20 years to neutralise. Outraged Bulgarians formed an 'eco-glasnost' pressure group – too late to affect the quality

The Danube at Ruse

The Danube at Ruse provides more eyesores than vistas, though it is vital to wildlife

of Danube water – but this group was part of the developing opposition movement that brought the end of communism in Bulgaria a year later.

Today, Bulgaria still doesn't sell its stretch of the Danube well. Lovers of industrial heritage will enjoy the toing and froing of the huge rusting hulks that carry coal along the river, but for most others there is little allure.

Surprisingly, the beacon of economic hope that membership of the European Union brings has also raised a conundrum for the Danube and for the EU's own reputation as friend to the environment. It is one of the EU's core policies to facilitate and promote the use of environmentally friendly forms of transport. Part of this is to get cargoes on to the water if at all possible and the Danube is seen as fundamental to this aim.

However, in a river plan announced in 2004 it was clear that the dredging and damming necessary would cause irreparable damage to the remaining marshlands along the river's path, and perhaps the loss of the Sreburna Nature Reserve. Environmentalists opposed the programme.

In 2010, Bulgaria was one of the 15 countries bordering the river to adopt the Danube River Basin Management Plan. This scheme outlines concrete measures, to be implemented by 2015, to improve the environmental condition of the river.

However, the full effects of the one million cubic metres of toxic red sludge, which spilled into the Danube after an industrial disaster in Ajka, Hungary in October 2010, could prove disastrous for both humans and wildlife in the years to come.

Getting away from it all

Bulgaria presents many and varied ways to get off the beaten track. Much of the country is unknown to mass tourism and it's easy to slip away from the mainstream, even in large towns. However, it is the country's unspoilt hinterland that is the real treasure. Opportunities for eco-tourism are excellent here, and the industry is in its infancy as Bulgaria concentrates on the economic recovery from the fall of communism and the adoption of a market economy.

Bulgaria's mountains

Pirin Planina (Pirin Mountains)

Nestling in the very southwestern corner of the country, the Pirin Mountains are famed throughout Bulgaria for their lakes and mineral springs, set among dramatic alpine cirques and surrounded by mountain peaks. Natsionalen Park Pirin (Pirin National Park), at 40,000 hectares (99,000 acres), is the largest in Bulgaria and is listed by UNESCO because of rare natural features such as tufa towers, the diversity of flora and fauna and the number of rare species, which include wild bears.

Though less well known to outsiders for its skiing (*see p101*), Pirin is internationally regarded for its excellent walking trails centred on its main resort Bansko, but also from Popina Luka, north of Sandanski in the heart of the range. A cross-range trip can take up to ten days, but shorter routes are also marked.

Pirin National Park Headquarters;
www.pirin.bg (in Bulgarian).
Pirin Tourist Forum. Tel: (0749) 88204.

Rila Planina (Rila Mountains)

The Rila Mountains, south of Sofia, are the Bulgarians' main playground, with excellent hiking in summer and the best-known resorts for winter sports. Almost every activity mentioned in the Sport and Leisure section (*see pp158–63*) is available here, but there's still enough space to find some peace and quiet.

Rila is a landscape shaped by glacial erosion. Crowned by Mount Musala, the highest peak in the Balkans and the sixth highest in Europe, the region offers landscapes from evergreen forests to alpine pastures and lakes; the upper elevations offer archetypal mountainscapes, many of which are protected by the 27,000-hectare (67,000-acre) Natsionalen Park Rila (Rila National Park).

The summer hiking trails are well marked but some of them are taxing for beginners because of their steep inclines. For good short trails – easy routes not too far from sources of refreshment – try Borovets (using the winter ski slopes routes) or the smaller resort of Maliovitsa. A network of routes can also be found around the famed Rila Monastery (*see pp90–92*). *Rila National Park Headquarters, ul. Bistritsa 12b, Blagoevgrad. Tel: (073) 880 537; www.rilanationalpark.org*

Rodopi Planina (Rodopi Mountains)

Forming Bulgaria's natural boundary with Greece to the south, the Rodopi Mountains lie in the heartland of the region known in antiquity as Thrace. The name is said by some to come from the pagan goddess Rhodope, though others say the range may be named from the Slavic words *ruda* and *ropa* meaning ore and pit, because mining has been an industry here since the Iron Age.

The range is generally lower in altitude than Pirin or Rila but is blanketed with expansive virgin pine forests in the north, and the karst and granite rocks have led to the formation of vast cave complexes and gorges.

The Rodopi see mild but snowy winters and warm but not hot summers, a climate that combines with the terrain to offer superb hiking and skiing, anchored by the internationally known resort of Pamporovo. It's also the area to go caving or potholing, and with rock formations such as Chudnite Mostove (Wonderful Bridges) it's good for climbing, too.

A typical view in the Pirin range

One of the 'Wonderful Bridges' in the Rodopi Mountains

Stara Planina (Stara Mountains)

The Stara Planina range (also known as the Balkan Mountain range) divides Bulgaria, running east–west through the middle of the country from the Serbian border to the Black Sea.
The range is the most ancient in the country: in fact its name is derived from a phrase meaning 'old mountain'. The range has been worn to little more than hills by millennia of erosion, but its highest peak, Mount Botev, rises to 2,376m (7,795ft) and it has several peaks over 2,000m (6,500ft), lying mostly in the western section.

The Stara Planina are the windiest mountains in Bulgaria, often forming the dividing line between two weather systems; this causes dangerous rushes of air through the mountain passes.

Unusually, rainfall is at its highest in June, with least rain falling in February.

It's less easy to get away from it all here, especially in the central section. The attraction is more in the hidden monasteries, traditional lifestyles and the generally more gentle gradients. However, there are two centres of excellence. The dramatic gorges at Vratsa and Iskur (*see pp52–3*) in the far west of the range (north of Sofia) are much loved by mountain- and free climbers and there are some great hiking trails cutting through the peaks. **Natsionalen Park Vrachanski Balkan** (Vrachanski Balkan National Park) was created in this same region (west of Vratsa) in the late 1980s to protect the karst landscape and 28,000 hectares (69,000 acres) of forested mountainscape, boasting over

700 species of flora and numerous natural caves.

Hiking possibilities are most comprehensive from the west, though there is a 650km (404-mile) marked route (the longest single route in Bulgaria) along the whole of the Stara Planina ridge (from Mount Kom to Cap Emine on the Black Sea), with regularly sited chalets. This can take over four weeks to complete.
Vrachanski Balkan National Park Information Centre, ul. Ivanka Boteva 1, Vratsa. Tel: (092) 660 318; www.vr-balkan.net; email: naturecenter@abv.bg. Open: daily 8am–4.30pm.

Other National Parks
Priroden Park Sinite Kamuni (Blue Rocks National Park)
The heart of rebel country during Bulgaria's fight for independence from the Turks, Blue Rocks protects a small,

BEAR SANCTUARY
There's been a tradition of dancing bears in the Balkans since the Middle Ages but sensibilities about performing animals have changed even here, and in 2002 the government made it illegal to 'exhibit' a bear.

Several owners came forward to hand in animals that were of no economic use, and with the help of the Brigitte Bardot Foundation, a 12-hectare (30-acre) sanctuary has been set up close to Belitsa in the Rila Mountains to rehabilitate and protect these unfortunate animals.

once impenetrable corner of the country. Today it's a 90-minute walk to the highest peak but there's also a chairlift for those who can't face the hike, and you can explore the caves that the revolutionary guerrillas used for almost two centuries.
Chairlift theoretically operates summer Tue–Sun 8.30am–5pm, Mon noon–5pm; reduced hours in winter. Admission charge.

Getting away from it all

Ancient hills of the Stara Planina

Priroden Park Zlatni Pyasutsi (Golden Sands National Park)

Fragrant pine forest extending over 1,300 hectares (3,200 acres) blankets the hillsides of the northern Black Sea coast and provides the perfect antidote to the bustle of the coastal resorts. An hour's walk through the heady aroma of pine is Aladzha Monastery (*see p116*), carved out of the rocks in the 12th century but long abandoned.

Priroden Rezervat Kaliakra (Kaliakra Nature Reserve)

Protecting vast expanses of the coastline, the boundaries of the 650-hectare (1,600-acre) reserve extend out into the shallows of the Black Sea to a distance of 500m (550yds). The area has become known as the Bay of Birds for its over 300 native and migratory species, though it is also home to a small number of dolphins and seals – the populations are now thought to be in single figures, so you are unlikely to catch a glimpse of either. The cape consists of high sheer cliffs with spectacular long-range views, but there is no safe access to the shoreline. Bring binoculars and you can enjoy hours of birdwatching, including breeding colonies clinging to the sheer rock face.

Those less enamoured with ornithology can explore the remains of the Kaliakra citadel, in use from the 4th century BC until the 17th century AD. Much of what still remains is Byzantine.

Kaliakra Information Centre on the main street in Bulgarevo (also spelt Bâlgarevo) village on the approach to the cape. Tel: (0574) 4424. Open: daily approximately 8am–6pm.

This ancient stone arch at Kaliakra provides a perfect lookout point

Kaliakra citadel has a spectacular position at the cliff edge

Priroden Rezervat Ropotamo (Ropotamo Nature Reserve)

One of Eastern Europe's most important marshland wildernesses, the Ropotamo protects 20km (12^1/$_2$ miles) of river mouth attracting over 250 species of birds. The sand dunes that separate the marshes from the open ocean are the most extensive in Bulgaria and they are also part of the reserve, forming an important habitat for flora that includes rare sand lilies.

A section of the Ropotamo is designated as parkland, offering short hiking trails and a boat trip along the river to catch a glimpse of the less shy wild creatures, including breeding colonies of egrets and herons, turtles and huge carp.

The Bulgarian–Swiss Biodiversity Conservation Programme (BSBCP) runs the reserve. www.bsbcp.biodiversity.bg

Priroden Park Rusenski Lom (Rusenski Lom Nature Park)

The three-pronged river valleys of the Rusenski Lom, Beli Lom and Malki Lom rivers form the Rusenski Lom National Park, one of Bulgaria's largest

Rusenski Lom is excellent hiking country

protected wildernesses. The sinuous park covers forested mountains, low rising hills and exceptional karst landscape. This range of natural environments has created a wide variety of habitats for over 170 species of native bird, including great eagle owls, more than 20 species of bat and over 60 other species of mammal, of which 16 are endangered. It also encompasses over 30 incredible rock-cut churches, of which Ivanovo Rock Monastery (*see p126*) is the highlight, and the second-largest cave in Bulgaria, the Orlova Chuka Peshtera (Eagle Peak Cave), just south of the village of Tabachka. The region offers hiking on less well-established routes than the mountain parks and a less formalised tourist infrastructure.

Information centres are located at the town hall in Ivanovo and at the National Park Office, ul. General Skobelev 7, Ruse. Tel: (082) 872 397; www.lomea.org

Priroden Reservat Sreburna (Sreburna Nature Reserve)
Listed as a World Heritage Site by UNESCO, Lake Sreburna (also spelt Srebârna) is a slow-flowing freshwater marsh, only 5m (16ft) deep at its maximum, that drains into the Danube. This shallow depth is the perfect environment for reeds and other water-loving plants, which in turn act as a magnet for waterbirds. Over 160 species inhabit the reserve, from ducks to cormorants, herons to pelicans. Several are on

the endangered list. Many nest on remote reed 'islands' that grow throughout the reserve away from the interference of man.

Priroden Park Strandzha (Strandjha Nature Park)

Established as recently as 1995, Strandjha sits on the very southern tip of the Black Sea coast, stretching to the Turkish border. Little visited because of its remote location, it offers a real chance to experience unspoilt and exceptionally varied landscapes from deciduous forest to excellent beaches and marshy shallows. With over 250 species of bird and over 60 species of mammals, it has the largest and most varied flora and fauna of any park in Bulgaria. The hiking here is easy because the terrain is flat and there are numerous trails ranging from 3km (1³/₄ miles) to over 20km (12¹/₂ miles).

For those more interested in history than in wildlife there are several ruined Byzantine citadels to explore, now languishing in the foliage. These constructions once formed part of a formidable defensive boundary.

There is little mainstream tourist infrastructure but camping is permitted within its boundaries (but with no facilities); this may be the way to see the park at its best. The village of Bulgari in the north of the park hosts a unique fire-walking festival in early June. Otherwise you'll have much of the Strandjha to yourselves.

Priroden Park Vitosha (Vitosha National Park)

See pp46–9.

Getting away from it all

Unspoilt Lake Sreburna, nesting place for many waterbirds

Birdwatching

With its exceptionally varied natural landscape and numerous protected regions, Bulgaria is Europe's richest country in terms of birdlife. In addition to its many native birds, the country lies on the direct route for many migratory species that make a pit stop here between their seasonal African and European homes. Around 400 species have been documented, but spring is the best time to visit for sheer variety, with an average of 220 species on Bulgarian soil.

Storks' nests are still common in many parts of Bulgaria

Plentiful species

This is the best place in the world to see wallcreepers (*Tichodroma muraria*), the biggest European populations of masked and lesser grey shrike (*Lanuis nubicus* and *Lanuis minor*), short-toed treecreeper (*Carthia brachydactyla*), Spanish sparrow (*Passer hispaniolensis*), collared flycatcher (*Ficedula parva*), black-headed and rock bunting (*Emberiza melanocephala* and *Emberiza cia*), black-headed wagtail (*Motacilla flava feldegg*), golden oriole (*Oriolus oriolus*), bee-eater (*Merops apiaster*), hoopoe (*Upupa epops*), rose-coloured starling (*Sturnus roseus*), corncrake (*Crex crex*), Syrian woodpecker (*Dendrocopos syriacus*), calandra and short-toed larks (*Melanocorypha calandra* and *Calandrella brachydactyla*) and rock nuthatch (*Sitta neumayer*).

Rare species

Species that are rare in the rest of Europe but more numerous here include the pallid swift (*Apus pallidus*), little and spotted crake (*Porzana parva* and *Porzana porzana*), stone curlew (*Burhinus oedicnemus*), collared pratincole (*Glareola pratincola*), gull-billed and Caspian tern (*Gelochelidon nilotica* and *Sterna caspia*), eagle owl (*Bubo bubo*), scops owl (*Otus scops*) and Tengmalm's owl (*Aegolius funereus*), shore lark (*Eremophila alpestris*), rock and blue-rock thrush (*Monticola saxatilis* and *Monticola solitarius*), barred, Sardinian and Orphean warbler (*Sylvia nisoria*, *Sylvia melanocephala* and *Sylvia hortensis*), nutcracker (*Nucifraga caryocatactes*), rock sparrow (*Petronia petronia*) and dotterel (*Charandrius morinellus*).

When and where to set up your hide

The Rodopi Mountains are Europe's richest environment for raptor species, autumn being the best time to see them. There are said to be 20,000 common buzzards (*Buteo buteo*), 6,000 honey buzzards (*Pernis apivorus*), 10,000 lesser-spotted eagles (*Aquila pomarina*) and a handful of rare Lammergeyer (*Gypaetus barbatus*) scanning the countryside for a tasty mouse or vole.

From August to October you'll be witness to a magnificent show of bird migration around the Burgas Lakes – white and black stork (*Ciconia ciconia* and *Ciconia nigra*), white pelican (*Pelecanus onocrotalus*) and short-toed eagle (*Circaetus gallicus*), all heading south to winter quarters.

Winter is the time for the goose family from the north, especially in northern Bulgaria at Lake Shabla. Here you'll find healthy populations of the white-fronted, lesser white-fronted, red-breasted and greylag goose (*Anser albifrons*, *Anser erythropus*, *Branta ruficollis* and *Anser anser*).

Sreburna Reserve in northeastern Bulgaria, just south of the Danube, has the largest colony of Dalmatian pelican (*Pelicanus crispus*) in Europe, at 220 pairs. There are just 20 pairs of imperial eagle (*Aquila heliaca*), but numerous glossy ibis (*Plegadis falcinellus*), booted eagle (*Hieraaetus pennatus*) and chukar (*Alectoris chukar*) are to be found.

Useful organisations

Information and activities for birdwatchers with affiliations to international organisations:
The Royal Society for the Protection of Birds (RSPB), The Lodge, Sandy, Beds, SG19 2DL, United Kingdom. *Tel: +44 (0)1767 680551; www.rspb.org.uk*
Holidays for lovers of nature, all run by a professional biologist:
Pandion D, 20A bul. Cherni Vrah, Sofia. *Tel/fax: (02) 963 0436; www.birdwatchingholidays.com*
An extremely useful book is *Finding Birds in Bulgaria*, by Dave Gosney (easybirder, 2010).

Shopping

Bulgaria has an exceptional range of arts and handicrafts that make excellent souvenirs. Prices range from very cheap for mass-produced items to thousands of pounds or dollars for unique pieces. The only difficulty you may have is in making a final choice and having enough room in your suitcase for all your purchases – watch your luggage allowance!

WHAT TO BUY

The two most widespread options are colourful patterned pottery, and lace and crocheted items handmade by a veritable army of ladies, whose hands are at work even as they mind their stalls. Other interesting items are woven carpets and fabrics, carved wooden objects, icons, Russian dolls, jewellery made from shells, coral and semi-precious stones, wine, spirits, rose-scented foodstuffs and toiletries, art, antiques, communist and military memorabilia, and winter sports clothing and equipment.

WHERE TO BUY
Sofia

For open-air shopping head to the collectors' market in pl. Alexander Nevski, where you'll find old military souvenirs such as Russian medals, guns and swords. The alleyway between the square and the Military Club (on bul. Tsar Osvoboditel) is lined with stalls of art, while around the Alexander Nevski Church itself is the place to look at handmade lace. The book market on bul. Slaveikov is an excellent place to browse for souvenir guides but also first editions and second-hand editions in a range of languages. For general cheap and fun souvenirs try the underpass near the Sveta Petka Samardzhiiska Church and outside the Hali market. Western-style shops and boutiques are now commonplace in the larger or more touristed towns. Try bul. Vitosha, or what was once communist Sofia's largest department store, **TsUm**, on bul. Maria-Luiza (*tel: (02) 926 0700*).

There are several shops and galleries where you can buy the highest-quality handicrafts at commensurately high prices. *See also the galleries listed on page 154.*

Art Gallery Paris

A fast-revolving selection of local art is on sale at this small, friendly venue.
ul. Parizh 8. Tel: (02) 980 8093; www. gallery-paris.com. Open: Mon–Fri 11am–2pm & 2.30–6.30pm, Sat 11am–2pm.

Ethnological Museum Shop

Textiles, kilims, masks, icons, ceramics, jewellery, folk music and copies of museum pieces.

ul. Paris 4 and pl. Battenberg 2 (in the Ethnological Museum).
Tel: (02) 987 4191.

Gaya Gallery

Paintings, ceramics and mobiles by young artists selling their work for the first time. The shop next door is also worth a visit for its home-made jewellery. Ul. Krakra is around the corner from the Crystal Palace hotel.
ul. Krakra 19. Tel: (02) 943 3591. Open: Mon–Fri 11am–7pm; Sat 11am–5pm.

The Icon Museum

Good-quality modern icons. Many are copies of the originals in the museum.
Crypt of Alexander Nevski Church, pl. Alexander Nevski.
Tel: (02) 988 1704.

Mirella Bratova

Designer Mirella Bratova turns out smart garments for women in linen and silk and some beautiful tops using Thai silk.
ul. Tsar Shishman St 4.
www.mirellabratova.com;
tel: (02) 943 5420. Open: Mon–Fri 10.30am–8pm; Sat 10.30am–6pm.

Central Bulgaria
Etur

Though it's not a huge complex, Etur has the full range of Bulgarian handicrafts, all fabricated by hand on site. You'll find a potter, weaver, leather-tooler, jeweller, woodcarver and icon painter within the complex. All are

Icon shopping in Sofia

Arbanasi handicrafts

masters of their craft so prices are higher than for the mass-produced equivalent.
7km (4 miles) southeast of Gabrovo. Tel: (066) 801 830.

Koprivshtitsa and Tryavna

Koprivshtitsa is a little disappointing for shopping. There are a few souvenir shops and stalls around the main square selling lace and handicrafts. However, the streets of Tryavna have a good range of shops selling woodcarvings from simple bowls to ornate picture frames, pottery and locally produced art.

Kotel

If you have a particular interest in carpets, head to Kotel, where they are still handmade. Though there are no shops in town, the **Carpet Exhibition Hall** has a range on sale.
ul. Izvorska 17. Tel: (0453) 2316. Open: summer Mon–Fri 9am–6pm; winter Mon–Fri 8am–noon & 1–5pm.

Oreshak

The Exhibition of Applied Arts and Traditional Crafts Complex is a rather ugly modern building, but at the same

time a repository that houses a comprehensive range of handmade and mass-produced souvenirs.
On the road to Troyan Monastery. Tel: (0670) 22062.

Southwestern Bulgaria

Plovdiv offers the largest range of shopping in the region. The old town has several dozen antique shops, many congregated on ul. Saborna, where you can pick up period lace, old photographs, war memorabilia or interesting communist-era items. All along ul. Saborna, stalls sell traditional pottery, and artists use the railings to set up impromptu gallery space. More artists congregate around the Dzumaya Mosque – you'll get the full range from icons to abstract art. High-street shopping is best on pedestrianised bul. Alexander Battenberg.

Melnik is the place to buy wine. A host of shops and stalls sell locally produced labels along with local foodstuffs such as honey and jam. Treated sheepskins make excellent rugs.

The winter resorts of Pamporovo and Borovets offer competitive prices on winter sports equipment, especially at the end of the season. In summer an array of traditional lace and summer clothing takes the place of skis and poles.

Sadly the major monasteries don't have much in the way of good-quality souvenirs, concentrating mainly on mass-produced or lower-quality icons and religious items. You'll normally find a handful of souvenir stalls outside the gates – the largest selection sits outside Bachkovo.

The Black Sea coast

The Stariyat Dobrich Complex is a good place to admire a range of Bulgarian handcrafted souvenirs, and prices are reasonable. However, the choice doesn't come close to matching what you'd find on the streets of Nesebur, with its wealth of small galleries, pottery emporia and little shops whose walls are swathed in lace, or to a lesser extent Sozopol.

At Balchik, an extensive crafts 'market' has set up on the approach to the Summer Palace of Queen Marie – with some excellent traditional pottery, interesting jewellery and art. Prices are a little higher than elsewhere in the region because of the palace's popularity with tour groups.

There's a great collection of lace displayed outside the cathedral in Varna.

The major coastal resorts – Albena, Golden Sands and Sunny Beach – all have a range of souvenir shops and stalls.

COUNTERFEITERS

At Ladies' Market and the Book Market in Sofia (and in markets all across the country) you'll find counterfeit CDs and DVDs at a fraction of the cost of the genuine article. The prices may be tempting, but you've no guarantee that they'll play on your machine when you get home, and no guarantee of quality of the contents, indeed no guarantee that you'll actually get what's on the label.

Icons

Traditional methods of icon painting are slow and painstaking

Icons are one of the most outstanding features of Orthodox Christian worship. Stylised depictions of Christ or of a venerated saint, they form the focus of worship because they are believed to be imbued with the Holy Spirit, and so are a direct conduit to heaven, with the ability to answer prayers and grant wishes. Believers pay homage to the icon, lighting candles to or even kissing the painting before making silent entreaties for strength, hope or courage in facing life's daily tribulations.

A number of icons are legendary, believed to be imbued with miraculous powers to save communities from famine, pestilence and war. They will normally be paraded through the streets on the saint's day at the head of a large procession, to bring luck to the population in the coming year. In addition to this, each saint has his or her own particular jurisdiction, acting as a spokesperson in the afterlife for farmers, fishermen, the sick or the infertile, for instance.

Icon painting began with the rise of the Eastern Christian or Byzantine Church at Constantinople after AD 330. The Orthodox form of Christianity spread north through the Balkans into Russia, southwest to Greece and southeast into Turkey and Syria as Byzantine religious influence and political power reached its zenith at around the time of the first millennium. Icon painting was the primary art form of Byzantium, a genre with complicated rules on form and style, requiring use of the finest pure pigments, precious metals and even precious stones. But with the spread of Islam on the back of the expansion of the Ottoman Empire, icon painting became a clandestine activity concentrated in the monastery complexes.

Creating an icon

Traditional methods of creating an icon painting are time-consuming, requiring patience to work through the various processes and time to build up the layers of colour necessary to produce the finished results. Consequently, authentically painted modern icons are not cheap.

The painter starts with a panel of wood cut to the appropriate finished size, to which is fixed a fine cotton cloth or gauze, using rabbit skin glue, which is allowed to dry. Then rabbit skin glue is heated with water and powder to make a gesso (a hard compound used as a base) and several thin coats of gesso are applied over the cloth to build up a base.

Though the genuine article is not cheap, a hand-painted icon makes a wonderful souvenir of Bulgaria

Each coat is allowed to dry before applying the next. Then the top layer is sanded with a fine glass paper for a smooth base.

The painter prepares a sketch of the final image on paper and draws an outline of this finished image on the panel. The panel is gilded by applying several layers of shellac (the resin of the lac insect), on top of which is added a layer of mixion (gold glue) and 23-carat gold leaf.

Painting can now begin. A tempera (water mixed with egg yolk and vinegar) is mixed as a base. This will be combined with various natural minerals to create the vivid colours. These paints are applied in numerous thin layers to create depth of colour. The halo of gold leaf is the last to be applied. In Bulgarian icon painting the halo traditionally has an embossed profile and this is achieved by applying natural resins to the surface. The icon is left for many weeks for the colours to settle before the final varnish is applied.

Icon studio

This studio produces hand-painted icons in the traditional way. Prices start at around 70 leva for a 5 × 10cm (2 × 4in) icon. Bespoke icons of any size can be ordered and will be shipped.
Rossen Donchev, Etur.

Entertainment

The arts were well subsidised under the communist regime. Ticket prices were low and even relatively small towns had viable theatre companies. Today the subsidies have gone and ticket prices have had to be raised (though prices are still cheap by Western standards) and consequently audiences for the mainstream arts have fallen. This, combined with the fact that the younger generation now looks to Western pop culture, has caused the closure of some companies outside the capital.

That said, there are still centres of excellence and many worthwhile performances if you enjoy the classical arts. Sofia is the obvious high spot. It has an excellent and varied programme of exhibitions, along with respected opera, ballet and orchestral companies. But others include Plovdiv, Varna and Ruse, where you'll also find one or more experienced ballet, opera, theatre or orchestral companies. Bulgaria's numerous festivals include classical and arts performances, often in atmospheric outdoor venues such as parks or Roman amphitheatres.

Check out *www.programata.bg* for listings of current entertainment, nightlife and cultural events. Look out also for the free monthly *City Info Guide* (*cityinfoguide.net*).

Cinema, bars and club/discos are popular, and you'll find a thriving gambling scene with numerous casinos, often linked to the major hotels, especially along the Black Sea coast.

Out in the countryside it's a total contrast to the resorts and the capital. Some provincial towns will have music bars or a cinema, but otherwise your entertainment is confined to dinner and an early night.

The *Sofia Echo* (*www.sophiaecho.com*) provides up-to-date information on activities for the week ahead in its supplement with ticketing and timing information in English. It's published every Friday and you can find it in hotels and at newsstands. *The Insider's Guide* (*insidesofia.com*) is published four times a year and has a section on Culture and Leisure. It's available free at most hotels.

Information on events in Plovdiv can be found at *www.plovdivcityguide.com*

CLASSICAL PERFORMANCE VENUES

Bulgaria has several impressive late 19th-century opera/theatre venues that play host to both their own and touring companies. Sofia sees many international orchestral and opera companies.

Plovdiv

National Opera House

Opera and philarmonic performances.
pl. Tsentralen 1. Tel: (032) 625 553;
www.ofd-plovdiv.eu

Plovdiv Drama Theatre

Also called the Nikolai Masalitinov Drama Theatre. Stages mainly European classical performances including Shakespeare – however, performances are in Bulgarian (which could give *Romeo and Juliet* or *King Lear* a new twist if you already know the plot!).
ul. Knyaz Alexander Battenberg 38.
Tel: (032) 271 270;
www.dtp.bg; email: dtp@dtp.bg

Ruse

Ruse Opera

Hosts professional and amateur performances.

pl. Sveta Troitsa 7. Tel: (082) 825 037;
www.ofd-rousse.com.
Ticket office at ul. Alexandrovska 61.

Sofia

National Opera House

Home of the National Opera Company, and venue for touring companies. Full opera programme.
bul. Dondukov 30. Tel: (02) 987 1366;
www.operasofia.bg

Stara Zagora

Stara Zagora Opera

Visiting companies play here throughout the season (Oct–May).
bul. Tsar Simeon Veliki 108.
Tel: (042) 622 431;
www.stateopera-starazagora.com

Varna

Varna Opera

The most important house after Sofia, with a resident company.

Varna Opera House opened in 1947

pl. Nezavisimost. Tel: (052) 665 010;
www.operavarna.bg

CONCERTS

The classical concert programme is full
and varied, with Bulgarian and
international artists filling halls large and
small. Popular and modern music
concerts tend to be limited to the capital.
More and more international artists are
adding Sofia to their itinerary – though
tickets sell out fast for the legends of rock
and pop. Here are some major venues:

Albena

Albena Variety Theatre

Shows and spectacles throughout
the summer.
Albena Cultural Centre.

Plovdiv

Puppet Theatre

Bulgarian Puppet Theatre.
bul. Hristo Danov 14. Tel: (032) 623 275;
www.pptheatre.com

Roman Theatre

Renovated Roman theatre used during

An outdoor dance performance

the summer for concerts and other special events.
ul. Hemus.

Sofia

NDK National Palace of Culture
Fifteen different-sized halls for performances of all kinds. This is an indoor venue where international pop acts sometimes appear when they visit Bulgaria.
pl. Bulgaria 1. Tel: (02) 916 6369; www.ndk.bg

Bulgaria Hall
Home to the Sofia Philharmonic orchestra, with a large hall and a smaller chamber hall.
ul. Aksakov 1.
Tel: (ticket office) (02) 987 7656.

Varna

Festival and Congress Centre
Several function halls for concerts and presentations, including the Love is Folly International Film Festival.
bul. Slivnitsa 2.
Tel: (052) 685 000.

Open-Air Theatre, Sea Gardens
Often a venue in the summer arts festival for theatre performances and live music.

Palais de Culture (Festival Hall)
Hosts events for all Varna's festivals (the summer festival runs throughout the summer with concerts) and competitions. It also plays host to the Varna Film Festival in early September.
bul. Tsar Boris I 115.

CULTURAL INSTITUTES
Sofia has several cultural institutes. These hold regular exhibitions and concerts promoting their own national artists, plus regular social gatherings to promote cross-cultural understanding.

Sofia

British Council
ul. Krakra 7. Tel: (02) 942 4344; www.britishcouncil.org/bulgaria

Euro-Bulgarian Cultural Centre
bul. Stamboliiski 17. Tel: (02) 988 0084; www.eubcc.bg

French Cultural Gallery
ul. Diakon Ignatii 2. Tel: (02) 937 7922; www.institutfrance.bg

Italian Cultural Institute
ul. Alexander Zhendov 1.
Tel: (02) 817 0480; www.iicsofia.org

ARTS, FOLK AND CULTURAL EVENTS
Traditional music, song and dance together form one of the strongest elements of Bulgaria's collective cultural identity. You'll see these in some form at every domestic festival.

It's always worth asking your hotel receptionist or holiday rep about local festivals taking place during your stay. Even the smallest village has a couple of celebrations each year, and this is definitely one way to see Bulgarians having fun.

CINEMA
All major towns have cinema houses or multiscreen complexes. Films are

shown in the original language with Cyrillic subtitles, so provided you can ignore the stream of print at the bottom of the screen, it's easy to enjoy the latest Hollywood blockbusters in English.

Plovdiv
Cinema City
Plovdiv Mall, ul. Perushtica 8.
Tel: (032) 273 000; www.cinemacity.bg (in Bulgarian).
Flamingo Cinema
bul. 6 Sevtembri 128. Tel: (032) 644 004.
Orpheus Open-Air Movie Theatre
Sahat teppe. Tel: (032) 633 637.

Sofia
Arena Zapad
This 15-screen multiplex comes with all the accoutrements you'd expect.
bul. Todor Aleksandrov 64.
Tel: (02) 920 9999; www.kinoarena.com
Odeon
Golden classics are the visual fare at this old-school venue.
bul. Patriarh Evtimiy 1. Tel: (02) 989 2469; http://bnf.bg/bg/odeon/program

GALLERIES
Commercial galleries, representing up-and-coming Bulgarian artists, have grown in importance in Sofia.

Sofia
Art Alley Gallery
Bulgarian and international artwork for sale, based around exhibitions that tend to change every month or so.

ul. Gladstone 51a. Tel: (02) 986 7363. Email:artalley@abv.bg
Art Gallery Paris
An owner-run gallery, small in size but selling original work by a new generation of Bulgarian artists.
Ul. Parizh runs along the west side of Alexander Nevski Church and the shop is near the National Opera House.
ul. Parizh 8. Tel: (02) 980 8093; www.gallery-paris.com. Open: Mon–Fri 11am–2pm & 2.30–6pm. Sat 11am–2pm.
Gaya Gallery
Easy to find, around the corner from the Crystal Palace hotel, this neat little gallery retails paintings, ceramics and mobiles by young artists selling their work for the first time. The shop next door is also worth a visit for its home-made jewellery.
ul. Krakra 19. Tel: (02) 943 3591.
Open: Mon–Fri 11am–7pm, Sat 11am–5pm; Jul & Aug Mon–Sat 10.30am–8pm, possible break 2–4.30pm.
Noe Art Gallery
Quality Bulgarian artwork – paintings, wood and bronze carvings.
ul. Parizh 6. Tel: (02) 980 6941; www.gallerynoe.com. Open: Mon–Sat noon–6.30pm.

BARS AND CLUBS
Discos and clubs are popular in the big cities. However, this sector is particularly prone to change, with clubs opening up and going out of business within a season. All the large hotels offer a music venue of some kind. They are your best options in the

coastal resorts and the capital. The establishments mentioned here are all successful and long-standing venues.

Hisar
Sound Factory
Behind Panorama restaurant.
Tel: 0879 651 221. Open: daily
11.30pm–5am.

Plovdiv
Club Plazma
Long-standing house club that has welcomed a host of international guest DJs.
bul. Hristo Botev 82. Tel: 0888 033 055;
www.clubplazma.com
Infinity
Opposite Marmalad, Infinity has an Egyptian theme to its décor and is less relaxing but more sociable.
ul. Bratja Poulievi 4.
Tel: 0888 281 431.
Marmalad
Trendy, but a place where you can chill out or take to the dance floor at weekends.
ul. Bratja Poulievi 3.
Tel: (032) 631 834; email:
marmalad@evrocom.net

Sofia
Blaze
Stylish bar on two levels with good music and chill-out atmosphere.
ul. Slavanska 36. Tel: 0888 354 004.
Buddha Bar
Oriental theme bar that has live music and DJs.

ul. Lege 15a. Tel: (02) 989 5006.
Open: 24 hours.
Escape
The city's top nightclub with international DJs.
ul. Angel Kanchev 1. Tel: 0889 990 000;
www.clubescape.bg
My Mojito
Popular club with DJs spinning cool sounds; good cocktails.
ul. Ivan Vazov 12. Tel: 0895 490 691.
Open: daily 9pm–5am.
O! Shipka
The main venue for live indie and alternative music.
ul. Shipka 11. Tel: (02) 988 2221.
Piano Bar Jack
Live piano music nightly.
ul. Rakovski 98. Tel: (02) 987 9198.
Toucan Bluzz & Rock
Live rock'n'roll, blues and jazz, Wednesday to Saturday nights; food available.
ul. Rakovski 112.
Tel: 0887 098 164; email:
emil_rock@abv.bg

Varna
Planet Club
Brit-style house music, open 24 hours.
bul. Tsar Simeon 1. Tel: 0897 886 978;
www.planetclub-bg.com
Tari Beer House
One of the most popular late-night haunts in Varna; contemporary rock music from 10pm until 2am.
bul. Slivnitsa 22.
Tel: (052) 610 269.

Children

Bulgaria is not particularly set up for children, but that is not to say it's not child-friendly. It's more perhaps that because children are freer to play in the old-fashioned sense than they are now in the West, they are often left to make their own entertainment. The attitude to children is positive. They stay out late, are welcomed at restaurants, and boisterous behaviour is generally indulged rather than frowned upon.

Though there are few specific attractions for children, Bulgaria has some advantages. The town and city centres will usually have a core of traffic-free streets where you won't need to keep your kids glued to your side for fear of their getting run over. Most towns and cities have areas of parkland and shady squares where kids can let off steam. Many parks have a small collection of child-sized battery-powered coin-operated cars and trucks, but few have swings and slides. Popcorn and candyfloss sellers cater to even the largest appetites.

Where for kids

The Black Sea

The Black Sea resorts are by far the most child-friendly areas for activities. Of course the beaches keep children of all ages happy throughout the day, but top that with a good range of watersports, small funfairs at each of the resorts, a couple of bowling alleys and karting tracks for older kids

and you have something for the whole family.

Most three-star hotels and above have decent-sized pools, and four-star hotels normally offer communal entertainment. Dedicated 'kids' clubs' are becoming increasingly common as the tourism industry develops.

There's always something to fill the evenings in every resort. The streets are lined with shops and stalls offering face painting, temporary henna tattoos and hair braiding, or old fairground-style games of chance. There's even the opportunity to have your picture taken in Victorian or other historical costume.

Sofia

Sofia's parks offer open space and there is a play area in **Borisova Gradina**. **Mount Vitosha** will engage energetic children keen to try some skiing, and trips on the chairlift and cable car should be fun. Cinema screenings are worth checking for suitable films,

and the **Galaxy Bowling Alley**
(*bul. Bulgaria 1; tel: (02) 916 6590*)
offers fun for all the family.

The popular Sunday brunch at
Flannagan's in the Radisson hotel
(*www.sofiaradissonsas.com*) has a
children's buffet and there is a
supervised children's area with video
screenings.

What for kids
Festivities and saints' days
There's always a festival going on
somewhere in Bulgaria and there's
nothing that children love more
than a parade, be it merry or
sombre. Folk dancing in traditional
costume is a major form of cultural
expression, and as Bulgarian children
are enthusiastic members of dance
troupes this enthusiasm is bound to
rub off on visiting children. There's
always an associated fair with rides,
market stalls and snacks. There
should be enough going on to fill
the whole day.

Skiing and snowboarding
The majority of ski runs in Bulgarian
resorts are greens and blues, ideal
for young children just starting out.
Packages to Bulgaria are good value,
making it the perfect place for a first-
time trip or a taster holiday.

Action Aquapark in Sunny Beach

Sport and leisure

Bulgaria offers myriad rural sports and leisure pursuits, from birdwatching to mountaineering. The mountain ranges are also home to several good-value ski resorts, while the freshwater lakes and extensive river system are best seen from a canoe. With the Black Sea coast offering a selection of watersports, there is every opportunity to keep active while on holiday.

Spectator sports

Bulgaria has a couple of organised sports that visitors may want to see, though this is one area of life that has suffered greatly since the programmes of the communist era ended.

Alpine and cross-country skiing

Bulgaria has played host to a handful of alpine skiing races. To see what's on during any particular season consult the Fédération Internationale du Ski (FIS) (*www.fis-ski.com*).

Levski Sofia's home ground

Football (soccer)

Like much of the world, Bulgarians take their football much more seriously than their politics. Their league is not one of the strongest in Europe but their two most successful clubs are the Sofia-based **CSKA** (*www.cska.bg*) and **Levski** (*www.levski.bg*). Both have made several forays into European competition.

Participation sports and leisure activities

Bulgaria is beginning to develop its leisure activity provision as tourism grows in importance, but is somewhat limited by a lack of modern equipment, few places to hire equipment and few competent English-speaking instructors. However, for already experienced sports people it offers new and exciting playgrounds for some activities, and two of its major strengths in leisure activities (birdwatching and hiking) require no technical expertise at all.

Odysseia Travel specialises in a full range of sporting and activity tours/holidays in Bulgaria and can help you plan and book a trip (*www.odysseia-in.com*).

Birdwatching

With swathes of pristine countryside and a vast range of divergent natural habitats, Bulgaria offers abundant opportunity for twitchers. Over 400 species call the place home or pass through on regular migratory journeys, stopping for a few days to re-energise,

Bulgaria is one of Europe's best destinations for birdwatching

and the country has several internationally important protected areas with over 150 species regularly on view (*see pp142–3*).

Canoeing and kayaking

With myriad freshwater lakes, and well-developed river systems to enjoy, it is no surprise that canoeing and kayaking are popular activities here, particularly in the spring when water levels are high with the meltwater from the mountain snows. However, equipment hire isn't widespread and it's not always easy to find competent tuition in English if you are a beginner. Several of the restaurants on the banks of Lake Iskur rent out kayaks and pedalos by the hour or day.

Make sure that you have life jackets – particularly for children.

Good walking country: Lake Dospat in the Rodopi Mountains

Hiking

Bulgaria is an exceptional destination
for hikers. With outstanding scenery,
well-marked footpaths and a network
of mountain huts offering simple
accommodation, it's possible to extend
hikes over hundreds of kilometres and
to spend weeks walking a route; this
is a complete alternative to the Sofia
city break or Black Sea beach type
of holiday.

Numerous short day-hikes of
between 1 and 20km ($^2/_3$ and $12^1/_2$
miles) can be found in the Vitosha
National Park just south of Sofia, the
Rila Mountains in the southwest, Pirin

HIKING MAPS

Domino (*www.domino.bg*) produces a range
of maps of the various National Parks
showing the walking and hiking routes,
though they are printed in Cyrillic. The best
range of these is available at the book market
on bul. Graf Ignatiev in Sofia.

Mountains, Rodopi Mountains and the central Stara Planina range. For more on national parks, *see pp134–41*. You can pick a route to suit your pace and fitness level; all you require is sturdy footwear and appropriate clothing for the weather conditions.

Trails are marked by coloured signs that correspond to plotted routes on good maps (*see box opposite*). These are easy to follow, requiring no specialist navigation skills.

The **Bulgarian Association for Rural & Ecological Tourism** (BARET; *www.en.baret-bg.org*) is responsible for instigating a number of ecotrails either through some of Bulgaria's most notable countryside or incorporating its most famous monuments. These include a route from Dryanovo Monastery and one in Vrachanska Balkan National Park.

Bulgaria has over 300 mountain huts on longer-distance and more challenging routes offering basic overnight accommodation, warm food and sanitary facilities. For details about booking huts *tel: (02) 980 1285*.

Horse riding

The slow pace of trekking on horseback is excellent for wandering through the Bulgarian countryside and is becoming an increasingly popular option at the major tourist hotspots. For those with no experience, however, there are few places to get lessons in English.

The forests of Borovets offer excellent trails in the summer.

INSURANCE

Some of the sports and activities suggested here may not be covered by a standard travel insurance policy. Always check with your insurance company that you are covered before heading out to Bulgaria, or, alternatively, check that the company you are organising the activity with has liability cover in the event of an accident.

Pamporovo also has provision in summer – choose from a selection waiting around the central junction of the town. A location with a more organised setup is the Arbanasi Horse Base in Arbanasi in central Bulgaria. For more information: *www.horseridingbulgaria.com*

Mountain biking

Increasingly popular along the hiking routes all across Bulgaria, mountain biking is limited at the moment because of a lack of places to rent equipment. The easiest places are at the ski resorts, where the winter pistes become summer trails and you can rent equipment at Mount Vitosha, Borovets and Pamporovo.

Mountain biking is particularly easy in the Stara Planina, where tourist offices affiliated with the Association Stara Planina hire bikes by the hour or day – and gradients aren't as steep as on Vitosha.

An initiative with Swiss assistance has designated a series of mountain bike tracks around Troyan, Gabrovo and Teteven with rides of different lengths and ability levels, linking major

Bulgaria presents some challenges to the climber

the peaks over 2,000m (6,500ft) offer reasonable challenges for a more organised expedition.

The **Bulgarian Alpine Club** (*bul. Vassil Levski 75, Sofia. Tel: (02) 930 0532*) can offer information and useful assistance with arranging climbs.

Potholing

Blessed with some exceptionally fine cave systems – over 4,000 documented caverns and potholes, the longest being over 15km (9 miles) long, the deepest at 415m (1,360ft) – Bulgaria offers challenges for even the most experienced caver. The best sites are in the karst regions west of Vratsa, in the western Rodopi Mountains and the Pirin karst.

Beginners are not well catered for and are advised to enjoy the guided tours of some of the larger cave complexes mentioned in the main section of this guide rather than head underground alone.

Scuba diving

Scuba diving is not as widespread along the Black Sea coast as one might expect, so Bulgaria might not be the place to get your initial certification; there are few instructors who can speak English and few places to hire equipment if you already have certification. This situation is gradually improving.

Skiing

See pp100–101.

tourist attractions to form a tour of several days. Maps are available at tourist offices in each of the towns. You can also rent a bike and a guide if you want one.

Mountaineering and climbing

Bulgaria's mountains make an excellent playground for the experienced climber. The birthplace of the sport, the Iskur Gorge, is still popular, while Maliovitsa in the Rila Mountains is a centre of excellence, with several alpine peaks close by. The serrated surfaces of White Rocks National Park attract free climbers and mountaineers for their short, testing ascents, while several of

Spas and therapeutic treatments
See pp164–5.

Watersports
When it comes to watersports, Albena is the nation's capital. This purpose-built resort offers everything that the enthusiast of any age would want, from banana-boat rides to waterskiing, windsurfing and jet-skiing. Numerous kiosks on the beachfront offer equipment rental but not instruction.

Watersports, but not necessarily the whole range, are also available at Golden Sands, Sunny Beach, Sozopol, Pomorie, Primorsko and Dyuni along the Black Sea coast.

The Black Sea coast is well developed for watersports

Spa treatments

Well-being is an ever-growing passion in much of the modern world, where a little pampering seems to have transcended the barrier from luxury item to human right. Today, the spa is the place to be seen enjoying a plethora of non-invasive cosmetic procedures. If you are looking for somewhere different to spend a little down time, try Bulgaria.

The country has an exceptional wealth of natural mineral springs, hot springs and beneficial mud that have been the basis of treatments for centuries. The Greeks and particularly the Romans had a love of bathing – it was almost as much about socialising as cleanliness. Some of the most renowned spas in the Roman Empire were in Bulgaria at Hisar, Sandanski, Sliven and Burgas – these were further developed as the Roman Empire gave way to the Byzantine.

During Ottoman rule, the Islamic precept of cleanliness drove further development of huge baths complexes open to all, and the newly independent Bulgaria was inaugurated at about the same time as 19th-century Europe discovered

The luxurious spa at Sunset Resort in Pomorie

complementary medicines. Doctors would happily prescribe a sojourn in the mountains and on the coast as a treatment for a range of conditions. Grand spas such as that at Sveti Konstantin in Bulgaria were filled with guests from royalty to the new glitterati – writers, composers and playwrights.

Though Westerners disappeared from the spas of Bulgaria during the communist era, Russians took their places in vast numbers. The population became used to being prescribed complementary therapies as part of an underfunded and non-innovative health service, so much so that they were regarded as mainstream treatments for skin disorders, high blood pressure, breathing problems, arthritis, nervous conditions and kidney and liver complaints.

Today there are over 500 balneotherapy centres in Bulgaria, and 250 thermal sources. Each offers a different speciality and some only deal with medical cases. The most developed pleasure spas can be found on the Black Sea coast at Albena, Sunny Beach, Golden Sands and Sveti Konstantin. A useful source of information is the **Bulgarian Association of Balneotourism** (*bul. Peio Yavorov 40, 8200 Pomorie. Tel: (0596) 25866; http://bab-bg.eu*).

The town with the largest number of mineral springs in Bulgaria is Velingrad, with over 70. The hottest spring is the one in Sapereva Banya near Dupnitsa, with a constant temperature of 40°C (104°F). It is claimed to be the hottest in Europe.

A quick guide to spa treatments
Aromatherapy – use of essential oils to improve mood or ameliorate minor conditions.
Detox or detoxification – the process of removing toxins – substances that are damaging or poisonous, such as caffeine or alcohol, from the body.
Exfoliation – removal of the upper layers of the epidermis to eliminate toxins and promote new skin growth.
Helio-prophylaxis – sunlight therapy.
Inhalations – for lung problems and for re-oxygenation of the system.
Mud treatments – to infuse minerals into or leach toxins out of the skin.
Ozone and oxygen therapy – like an ozone 'sauna' to eliminate free radicals.
Reflexology – the belief that areas of the feet are linked to areas of the body. Massage of these points promotes improvement in problem areas of the body.
Seaweed wrap – the body is coated in seaweed extract to re-mineralise and rehydrate the skin.
Thalassotherapy – use of seawater for massage.

Food and drink

Eating out in Bulgaria can be a pleasure. Food is delicious and cheap (bearing in mind the caveat Tourists Beware, see box opposite), although the impenetrable barrier to foreigners, the Cyrillic alphabet, still presents some problems with menus. But don't let a small challenge with language spoil your exploration of Bulgarian cuisine.

Where to eat

You'll find a range of eateries available in Bulgaria. The self-service cafeteria allows you to point at what you want rather than having to work your way through the menu. Cafeterias also offer excellent value and tasty fare.

A *mehana* is a Bulgarian tavern where waiters wear traditional costumes. Vegetarian restaurants are rare but non-meat dishes can be found on most menus – if this is in English, you will not have a problem.

What to eat
Bulgarian dishes

Bulgarian cuisine has influences from both Greece and Turkey and comprises a range of delicious summer and winter dishes. In winter Bulgarians start with

SIDE DISHES

You must order all side dishes (bread, vegetables, potatoes) separately from your meat, chicken or fish, and there will be a charge for each item.

a hearty soup, perhaps *bob* (bean soup) or *topcheta supa* (soup with meatballs). In summer, salad is favoured, normally the *shopska salata* (tomatoes, cucumber and onion topped with grated cheese), which can be found just about everywhere. A small range of starter dishes or dips can also be ordered including *tarator* (yoghurt soup with cucumber and walnuts), *mletcha salata* (yoghurt with cucumber, walnuts and garlic), *sarmi* (vine or cabbage leaves stuffed with rice and spices, sometimes with meat) or *kashkaval pane* (breaded fried cheese).

The basis of most main courses is simple grilled meats – chops, ribs and steaks. *Meshana skara*, the Bulgarian equivalent of a mixed grill, is a popular choice. Other items include *kebabche*, a grilled spicy sausage, and *kyufke*, a spicy meat patty.

Bulgarians also have a delicious range of slow-cooked dishes, including their national dish *kavarma* (a slowly cooked stew of pork and liver), *drob sarma* (chopped liver, rice and eggs baked in the oven) and *sirene po shopski* (eggs and cheese baked in a clay pot with tomatoes). *Musaka* could be mistaken for the Greek moussaka but doesn't contain aubergine. If you work out the word *gyuvech* on the menu you'll be ordering meat stew.

Fish is popular along the Black Sea coast but will always be more expensive than meat. *Plakiya* is a delicious fish stew with no written recipe – just made with whatever was caught that day.

Bulgarians like to start the day with a *banitsa*, a warm pastry filled with cheese.

International cuisine

The large five-star hotels generally have a high-class restaurant serving international and continental cuisine at high prices. Chinese restaurants are numerous, along with Italian restaurants and pizzerias.

At the other end of the scale the international fast-food chains have certainly made their presence felt, while the Bulgarian chain Happy Bar and Grill serves good-value Western-style dishes. This network has also embraced the sushi craze, which has recently swept the more cosmopolitan areas of the country.

Drinks

Although drinking tap water is said to be safe, bottled water will certainly taste better. The short shot of strong coffee (espresso style) oils the wheels of Bulgarian society; it is available everywhere and is excellent. Bulgarians drink *bilkov* (herbal) or *plodov* (fruit) teas. Fresh fruit juices are a highlight of the summer, while the international brands of pop (soda) are readily available.

Bulgarian wine (*see pp172–3*) is well regarded. The country also brews good beer; leading brands include Kamenitsa and Zagorka. For something with more oomph, try domestic brands of vodka, excellent *slivova rakiya* (plum brandy) and *rosaliika* (rose liqueur). International liquor favourites are available but at a price premium.

A useful phrase to end with – *Na Zdrave* means 'Cheers'.

Bulgarian food has a strong affinity with Greek and Turkish cuisine

Food and drink

The ★ sign indicates the price of a three-course meal without wine.

★   Up to 20 leva
★★   from 20–30 leva
★★★   from 30–40 leva
★★★★ over 40 leva

SOFIA
Central Hali ★
A food court on the top floor of a restored market hall. There's a coffee bar on the ground floor.
Corner of Maria-Luiza and ul. Ekzarh Yosif. Email: c-hali@bulinfo.net. Open: food court 9am–midnight, coffee bar 7am–midnight.

Happy Bar & Grill ★–★★
Neon-lit guitars and film posters on the walls, with laminated menus featuring grills, chicken, sushi and salads. Cheap and cheerful.
pl. Sveta Nedelya 4. Tel: (02) 980 7353. (Another branch at bul. Rakovski 145.) Open: 24 hours.

Egur, Egur ★★
Armenian restaurant where the period wallpaper and varnished wood flooring evoke a homely and relaxing atmosphere. Starters include the Armenian sausages or *shtoratz* (fried aubergine rolls), followed by mostly meat-based dishes like *massis* (chicken stuffed with salmon and spinach).
ul. Dobrudzha 10 and another branch at ul. Sheinovo 18. Tel: (02) 989 3383. Open: noon–midnight.

Happy Sushi ★★
The reliable Happy chain of diners has gone into sushi in a big way. This outlet, which has a trendy black and white Asian aesthetic, has separate smoking and non-smoking sections.
bul. Rakovski 96, opposite the Russian Church. Tel: 0887 999 361. Open: noon–midnight.

Upstairs ★★
Easy to find, this arty and fashionable eatery offers meals and drinks throughout the day.
bul. Vitosha 18. Tel: (02) 989 9696. Open: Mon–Sat 9am–2am, Sun 10am–2am.

Victoria ★★
With a superb, central location, Victoria's spacious terrace is busy throughout the day. Known primarily as a decent pizzeria, its lengthy menu also includes pricier meat dishes, as well as pasta, soup and salads. There's another outlet at ul. Ivan Asen II 66.
bul. Tsar Osvoboditel 7. Tel: (02) 986 3200; www.victoria.bg. Open: 11am–11pm.

Da Vidi ★★–★★★
Now under new ownership and with slightly less prohibitive pricing, this swanky joint serves posh Mediterranean nosh such as tiger shrimps with Pernod and vegetables, with a few pasta options. The black and white décor is appropriately trendy.
ul. Dimitar Manov 17. Tel: 02 980 6746. Open: 10am–11pm.

Chevermeto ★★★
Traditional local dishes and wines with folk-music accompaniment.
bul. Cherny Vrah 31. Tel: (0885) 630 308. Open: noon–midnight.

Istanbul ★★★
With smoking pipes, Arabian rifles and swords

spicing up the décor, Istanbul offers an extensive and tempting menu of Lebanese and Turkish specialities. Themed dance is held in the evening. The Kempinski's other eateries include a panoramic restaurant and charming cake shop.
Kempinski Hotel Zografski, bul. James Bouchier.
Tel: (02) 969 2222;
www.kempinski.com.
Open: Mon–Sat 11.30am–11.30pm, closed Sun.

Kumbare ★★★

This bright and smart Greek taverna isn't cheap, but the food wins plaudits for its quality and authenticity, with the octopus a particular favourite. Hellenic classics can all be washed down with a glass of ouzo or retsina.
ul. Saborna 14, behind Sveta Nedelya Church.
Tel: (02) 981 1794;
www.kumbare.com.
Open: 11am–midnight.

Shades of Red ★★★★

Classy Shades of Red takes its name from its plush colour scheme, which has recently undergone an overhaul. Housed in a five-star hotel, some dishes will set you back a fair bit (by Sofia standards), but there are also more frugal pasta options.
Grand Hotel Sofia, ul. Gurko 1.
Tel: (02) 811 0930;
www.grandhotelsofia.bg.
Open: noon–11pm.

CENTRAL BULGARIA
Etur
Vuzrozhdeiska ★★

Serves good Bulgarian food during museum opening hours.
Museum Complex.
Tel: (066) 801 691.

Hisar
National Garden Restaurant ★★

Good Bulgarian food in a pretty courtyard garden setting.

Rabotno Vreme, ul. Gurko.
Tel: (0887) 663 228.
Open: 11am–midnight.

Koprivshtitsa
Chuchura ★

Traditional Bulgarian restaurant set by the river with quality food and a good atmosphere.
ul. Palaveev 66.
Tel: (07184) 2712.

Tryavna
Hotel Family ★★

The service is friendly and the prices reasonable at this amiable eatery, which also offers free wireless Internet. The covered decking area at the front is a good spot for people-watching.
ul. Angel Kanchev 40.
Tel: (0677) 66034, 0882 424 889;
www.hotelfamily.bg

A typical Bulgarian dish: roast chicken with vegetables

Starata Loza ★★

This charming restaurant in the old town serves Bulgarian and continental dishes.
ul. Slaveikov 44.
Tel: (0677) 64501; http://starata-loza.tryavna.biz

Veliko Turnovo

Saint George Tavern ★

Enjoy views of the Tsaravets Fortress as you sup on traditional Bulgarian fare, with cottage pie, fish and chips, jacket potatoes, chicken tikka masala and their like thrown in for the homesick.
ul. G Mamarchev 14.
Tel: (062) 601 109;
www.georgespub.com.
Open: 11am–11.30pm.

Starata Mehana ★

Tiny restaurant with simple but well-cooked Bulgarian fare and great views over the town.
ul. Stefan Stambolov.

Han Hadji Nikoli ★★★

This restaurant dates back to 1858, and service, décor and food all do credit to its pedigree. The inventive fare includes frogs' legs and rabbit. Go upmarket with the gourmet menu or stick

to the tried and trusted, such as pasta, lamb, beef or fish. Start the meal with wine tasting in the room next door.
Samovodska charshia 19.
Tel: (062) 651 291. Open: 7am–midnight or 1am.

SOUTHWEST BULGARIA
Bansko

Dedo Pene ★★

The best place to eat if you are seeking a Bulgarian atmosphere. On warm days, the courtyard setting is very inviting.
ul. Bujnov.
Tel: 0888 795 970;
www.dedopene.com

Melnik

Hotel Despot Slav ★★★★

Fine continental cuisine at a reasonable price in a dining room furnished in wrought iron.
Tel: (07437) 2271 or 2248.

Plovdiv

Diana ★

Abuzz with rustic Bulgarian charm, Diana offers an array of national and generic international dishes. Despite its size, it can still be difficult to get a table

in peak hours during high season. Part of a nuclear bunker near the bathrooms provides further Cold War curiosity value.
ul. Dondoukov 3.
Tel: (032) 623 027.
Open: 24 hours.

Gusto ★★

International food and Art Deco interior. There is a bar downstairs.
ul. Otetz Paisii 26.
Tel: (032) 623 711.
Open: 9am–1am.

Hebros ★★★★

An adherent of the Slow Food movement, this old-town hotel restaurant provides an adventurous menu where delicacies such as frogs' legs sit alongside more traditional Bulgarian staples. Though it's fairly pricey by local standards, the lunchtime set menu is excellent value.
ul. Konstantin Stoilov 51A. Tel: (032) 260 180;
www.hebros-hotel.com.
Open: 8am–11.30pm.

BLACK SEA COAST
Balchik

Regina Maria ★★–★★★

The lovely terrace that extends out over the sea

provides more than enough reason to visit this pleasant hotel eatery. There's a good range of seafood, and the odd surprise ingredient.
On the seafront.
Tel: (0896) 743 405.

Nesebur
Kapitanska Sreshta ★★★★
The best seafood restaurant along the southern coast always has a fresh selection of fish, lobster and imported Russian caviar.
ul. Mena.
Tel: (0554) 42124. Open: 10am–approx. 11pm.

Pomorie
Venezia ★★★–★★★★
One of four à la carte restaurants that form part of the Sunset Resort complex, Venezia prides itself on being a proper Italian restaurant rather than a mere pizzeria (and in case diners forget the origin, the place is done out in the red, white and green of the Italian tricolour). Seafood, naturally, features – try the calamari or the prawns – and there is a range of pasta options.

Nearby are the complex's fish, sushi and French restaurants.
Sunset Resort, ul Kniaz Boris I, Pomorie.
Tel: (0596) 36200;
www.sunsetresort.bg

Varna
Trops Kashta ★
For no frills and great value, this long-established self-service canteen chain is the place. Point at the traditional Bulgarian fare that whets your appetite and away you go.
ul. Knyaz Boris I.
Tel: (052) 600 484;
www.tropshouse.bg.
Open: 8 or 8.30am–9 or 10.30pm.

La Pastaria ★★
Tasty Italian food, served up in true old country style, right down to the red and white check tablecloths.
ul. Dragoman 45.
Tel: (052) 632 060;
www.lapastaria.net.
Open: 11am–11pm.

THE NORTH
Ruse
Leventa ★★★
Though the food and service are both top-

notch, Leventa is most striking for its location: a 19th-century Ottoman fort. The seven dining halls – which once entertained Fidel Castro – were renovated at length and in 2005 reopened with hand-painted frescoes and a winery.
ul. General Kutuzov.
Tel: (082) 862 880;
www.leventa-bg.net.
Open: 11am–midnight.

Vidin
Bononia ★
Large hotel restaurant serving up meaty Balkan staples. The outdoor seating affords pleasant park and river views.
ul. Bdin 2.
Tel: (094) 606 031.
Open: 10am–midnight.

Bulgarian wine

Bulgarian wine production started late. The Romans didn't seem to see the benefit of the country's fine soil, preferring warmer climes such as Greece and southern Italy for their vineyards. It was only as Rome gave way to Byzantium in the 6th century that vines were planted in the area around Melnik, but the Bulgars learned fast.

Not all of the country is suitable for wine production, but Bulgaria's deep mountain valleys, its very varied soil types and its mixture of weather systems combine to produce several excellent microclimates.

Much of the production was given over to domestic consumption until the communist era, when a successful export market grew quickly from the beginning of the 1970s. Before the fall of the regime the country was among the top ten wine exporters. Much of it arrived in UK off-licences. Bulgaria became renowned for its cheap hearty red *vin de table*, the staple reliable budget choice for millions of Brits.

Unfortunately, with the fall of the regime, the wine industry suffered the same problems as many Bulgarian industries – market forces didn't sit well on the newly independent managements' shoulders and exports dropped. The wine market was also changing and drinkers were demanding higher quality than Bulgarian producers could supply in the short term.

The most forward-thinking began a process of reinvestment, replacing old and more rustic domestic varieties of vine with internationally recognised varieties such as Merlot, Cabernet Sauvignon and Chardonnay.

In 2009 660,000 hectolitres (14.5 million gallons) of wine were exported. The best wineries are producing some well-respected wine, though there are still many quaffable, less expensive options to explore.

Bulgarian winemakers are steadily improving quality for the export market

Quality of wine

There are several levels of quality for Bulgarian wine.

The basic quality is table wine. This is always a blend of unspecified grape varieties and does not denote the origin of the wine.

Country wine is another blend, but this time only two grape varieties can be combined and these must be stated on the label.

Wines of Declared Geographical Origin (DGO) are made from a single grape variety within a specific geographical location. At present these constitute the majority of Bulgarian production.

Controlled Appellation of Origin (AOC) wines are classified in line with the French system of quality control. They have to be made of a specific grape variety in vineyards with specific yield limits per hectare within a denoted region.

DGO and AOC wines achieve reserve status if they have been aged in oak for more than three years for reds or two years for whites.

Grape varieties

For reds, the French grape varieties Merlot and Cabernet Sauvignon are being planted, but local red varieties include: Gamza, the most widespread grape, producing soft, fruity, light-bodied wine; Mavrud, producing full-bodied red that ages well; Melnik, mostly grown in the southeast, producing heavy reds that age well;

The wines of Melnik are highly regarded

and Pamid, the mainstay of much of the table wine.

Whites made from international grape varieties such as Chardonnay, Sauvignon Blanc and Riesling are available, but you may also find local varieties Misket, Ottonel and Diamat.

Labels to look for

The following wineries/regions have a high reputation:

Damiantza	St Nikola
Domaine Boyar	Slavyantsi
Haskovo	Suhindol
Rousse	Vini Sliven

Wine tours

Romantic Wine Tours (*ul. Buzludja 47, Sofia; tel: (02) 951 6466; fax: (02) 951 6466; www.romanticwinetours.com*) offers escorted wine tours around Bulgaria for individuals and groups.

Accommodation

Bulgaria has a wide range of accommodation possibilities, with even more springing up in recent years, though there is a great difference in provision between town and country. Five-star hotels are few and concentrated in the capital, but there is more provision at the four- and three-star level in the major towns and cities, and of course along the Black Sea coast, with concentrations at Albena, Sunny Beach and Golden Sands. See www.hotels-in-bulgaria.com

Beyond the major tourist centres, prices really drop, but most hotels fall into the three- and two-star categories. Many so-called hotels are surprisingly small, having as few as three rooms. For most forms of accommodation prices are good value compared with Western Europe, even though foreigners may be charged more than native Bulgarians.

Bed and breakfast is an excellent budget option throughout the country. Rooms will be simple but spotlessly clean, though they probably won't have private bathrooms. Private room prices per night can be well below 50 leva, and that includes breakfast. Many of the monasteries offer overnight accommodation to travellers – though it usually won't be in an authentic monk's cell.

There's little pressure on accommodation provision except at times of major festivals, when booking ahead is essential. The Black Sea coast is always full from late July to September, when a lot of hotels are commandeered by large tour groups. Out of season (October–May) the majority of the accommodation on the Black Sea closes completely, and it may be more difficult to find rooms in private homes across the country.

If you want to travel independently, without making bookings ahead, then you can use the services of the commercial information offices throughout the country. They act as agents for hotels and B&Bs, but some are more helpful then others.

The following list of suggested accommodation shows price ranges charged to non-Bulgarians for a double room per night including breakfast. Prices of upmarket hotels may be priced in euros.

- ★ budget, under 80 leva
- ★★ mid-range, 80–130 leva
- ★★★ expensive, 130–220 leva
- ★★★★ very expensive, over 220 leva

SOFIA

Be My Guest ★

A hostel with dorms and private doubles, funkily decorated and well placed for getting around the city centre.
ul. Ivan Vazov 13.
Tel: (02) 989 5092; www.
bemyguest-hostel.com

Internet Hostel ★

Located in the centre, offering private rooms and a decent kitchen, Internet access and a vegetarian restaurant in the same building.
2nd floor, ul. Alabin 50 (city end of bul. Vitosha).
Tel: (0889) 138 298;
email:
interhostel@yahoo.co.uk

Lozenetz ★★

A little way south of the city centre, this modern and stylish hotel benefits from an above-average restaurant and helpful staff. It has wireless Internet connection.
ul. Sv. Naum 23.
Tel: (02) 965 4444;
www.lozenetzhotel.com

Niky ★★

Located down a quiet street off bul. Vitosha, this neat hotel has good-value singles and doubles plus 16 suites with kitchenettes. Well managed and with a decent restaurant.
ul. Neofit Rilski 16.
Tel: (02) 952 3058;
www.hotel-niky.com

Crystal Palace ★★★

Boutique-style hotel in a good location, close to the centre and with bars and restaurants nearby. There are Internet connections in the bedrooms, an excellent restaurant and a health-and-fitness club with sauna.
ul. Shipska 14.
Tel: (02) 948 9488; www.
crystalpalace-sofia.com

Grand Hotel Sofia ★★★★

With an excellent downtown location within walking distance of many of the city's main attractions, the Grand Hotel offers stately, spacious and comfortable rooms, a stylish fitness centre and a luxurious ambience.
ul. Gurko 1.
Tel: (02) 811 0811;
www.grandhotelsofia.bg

Kempinski Hotel Zografski ★★★★

Sofia's largest five-star hotel is the top choice of visiting VIPs, and understandably so. From the verdant gardens in which it is set and fabulous views from the upper floors to the small details such as the home-made biscuits, the Kempinski Hotel Zografski oozes class.
bul. James Bouchier.
Tel: (02) 969 2222;
www.kempinski.com

CENTRAL BULGARIA

Kazanluk

Hotel Hadzhi Eminova Kashta ★

Built in traditional style in the centre of town, its rooms are simple and bathrooms are on the small side, but there's a good restaurant on site.
ul. Nikola Petkov 22.
Tel: (0431) 62595.

Koprivshtitsa

Sezoni Hotel ★

Clean rooms with modern facilities. No restaurant, but breakfast is included in the room rate and there is a pleasant garden.
ul. Doncho Vatah Voivoda 12.
Tel: (07184) 2155 or (0898) 348 868; email:
rado.montrail@mail.bg

Tryavna
Hotel Zograf ★
Set in the old town and opened in 2002, this hotel pays homage to the artisans of Tryavna, being decorated throughout with carved wood. There's a traditional inn on the premises.
ul. Slaveikov 1.
Tel: (0677) 64980;
www.zograf.tryavna.biz

Veliko Turnovo
Gurko ★★
A small characterful hotel on one of the cobbled streets of the old town, the Gurko has well-equipped modern rooms, with panoramic views of the town from its balconies. Excellent restaurant.
ul. Gurko 33.
Tel: (062) 627 838;
www.hotelgurko.hit.bg
Interhotel ★★–★★★
Fantastic gorge views and quiet, comfortable rooms are the draws at this centrally located hotel, housed in a communist-era building. The communal areas have free wireless Internet.
ul. Aleksandar Penchev 2.
Tel: (062) 601 000;
www.interhotelvt.bg

SOUTHWEST BULGARIA
Bansko
Dedo Pene ★★
Not the quietest place in town, being above a popular restaurant, but comfortable rooms, a sociable atmosphere and everywhere within walking distance.
ul. Bujnov 1.
Tel: (0749) 88348;
www.dedopene.com

Blagoevgrad
Kristo ★
Easily the best choice for a night's stay in Blagoevgrad, located in the Varosha, the old part of town, but a short stroll to the city's bars and restaurants. There are over 30 air-conditioned rooms, a restaurant and bar, and a sauna.
ul. Komitrov, Varosha.
Tel: (073) 880 444; email: hotel_kristo@abv.bg

Melnik
Hotel Despot Slav ★
This restored mansion sits at the end of the town. The rooms are not over-large, but the bathrooms are modern. There's a good restaurant in the hotel.
Tel: (07437) 248.

Pamporovo
Hotel Snezhanka ★★★
A reasonably priced option in what is a very expensive resort by Bulgarian standards, the Snezhanka is open all year. Designed like an alpine chalet, and the rooms are simply furnished. The restaurant serves high-class cuisine.
Tel: (03095) 8316.

Plovdiv
Hebros ★★★★
In the heart of old Plovdiv, the Hebros is one of a new breed of modern, charming hotels in which each room is individually and tastefully decorated, but the price is commensurately high.
ul. Stoilov 51.
Tel: (032) 260 180;
www.hebros-hotel.com
Novotel Plovdiv ★★★★
This 330-room hotel, part of the French Novotel chain, offers good-quality accommodation with a

large pool and several eateries.
ul. Zl Bojadgiev 2.
Tel: (032) 934 444;
www.novotel.com

BLACK SEA COAST
Balchik
Byala Kushta ★
Possibly the nicest place to stay in Balchik, facing the sea and with pleasant, well-kept rooms.
ul. Geo Milev 18.
Tel: (0579) 73822; email:
white_house_balchik
@yahoo.com

Burgas
Hotel Bulair ★
Modern hotel with well-furnished rooms but a little lacking in charm. A good base for touring the southern Black Sea.
ul. Bulair.
Tel: (056) 844 389;
www.hotelbulair.com

Dobrich
Hotel Bulgaria ★★
Large central hotel with spacious rooms and facilities such as pool, casino and fitness room.
pl. Svoboda.
Tel: (058) 600 226;
www.bulgaria-
dobrich.com

Nesebur
Prince Cyril Hotel ★★
In the heart of the old town and, unusually for this coast, open all year, the Prince Cyril is set in a rustic traditional Nesebur house, though the rooms are modern and comfortable.
ul. Slavianska.
Tel: (0554) 42220.

Varna
Alekta Hotel ★★
With great views of the sun rising over the Black Sea, it's well worth staying here if you can be sure of a room facing the sea.
Sv. Nikola area.
Tel: (052) 335 040;
www.alekta.hit.bg
Odessos Hotel ★★★
Large, good-quality hotel overlooking the Sea Gardens in the heart of Varna. A good base for touring the northern Black Sea.
bul. Slivnica 1.
Tel: (052) 640 300;
www-en.odessos-bg.com

THE NORTH
Belogradchik
Hotel Madona ★
Family-owned hotel with only three rooms, so it's

in demand; the Madona sits by a stream amid green surroundings. The family also runs a restaurant on site which is the perfect place to spend an evening.
ul. Hristo Botev 26.
Tel: (0936) 5546.

Ruse
Best Western Bistra & Galina ★★
Built to raise money for charity, this swish Best Western outlet has a new building, separate smoking and non-smoking floors and Internet access. The hotel is modern with nicely furnished rooms. Good restaurant.
ul. Asparukh 8.
Tel: (082) 823 344.

Vratsa
Valdi Palace Hotel ★
Though this central, communist-era hotel looks rather dour from the outside, inside things improve considerably. Rooms are clean and the staff are welcoming.
pl. Hristo Botev.
Tel: (092) 624 150.

Practical guide

Arriving

Entry formalities

EU citizens can enter Bulgaria with a passport or valid picture ID. Citizens of the USA, Canada, Australia and New Zealand can spend up to 90 days there without a visa. Nationals of other countries should consult the Bulgarian Embassy in their own country for visa information.

By air

The main airport of entry for scheduled flights is Sofia (*Tel: (02) 937 2212*), though there are international flights into Varna and Burgas on the Black Sea coast. All major European airlines fly scheduled services into Sofia several times each week. Wizzair also has flights.

British Airways (*www.britishairways.com*), **Malév** (*www.malev.com*), **Wizzair** (*www.wizzair.com*).

Bulgaria Air (*www.air.bg*) is the major Bulgarian carrier, offering a network of services to major cities throughout Europe.

There are no direct flights from the USA, Canada, Australia or New Zealand to Bulgaria, though Virgin Atlantic has a code-share scheme with Bulgaria Air. Multiple-ticket combinations for flights into Europe and onward to Bulgaria are possible, so it's best to consult a travel agent about the cheapest or most convenient route.

Charter flights are available in winter to Sofia and Plovdiv and in summer to Varna and Burgas as part of a skiing or Black Sea package tour. Some companies may be happy to offer a flight-only deal, but it's also advisable to check prices of flight/hotel packages, as these may offer good value when compared to booking separate flights and hotels.

Balkan Holidays (*www.balkanholidays.co.uk*) **Regent Holidays** (*www.regent-holidays.co.uk*).

By rail

There are various rail routes, but at the moment it is still not possible to buy a through train ticket to Sofia. However, after booking part of your journey online, it is usually easy enough to pay for the remaining segments en route. It will take about 24 hours to reach Budapest from London (Eurostar to Paris and on from there by sleeper via Vienna or Munich), and the last leg of the journey, Budapest–Sofia, will take that long again.

From Italy: daily trains run from Venice to Sofia on the old Orient Express route.

From Eastern Europe: train services run daily all year from Bucharest to Sofia through Ruse. Trains also run to Ruse from Burgas and Varna on the Black Sea coast, linking with a service through Bucharest, Budapest and Prague.

From Turkey: daily trains from Istanbul to Bucharest have stops in

Bulgaria at Stara Zagora, Veliko Turnovo and Ruse.

From Greece: daily trains between Thessalonika and Bucharest have stops in Bulgaria at Blagoevgrad, Sofia, Pleven and Ruse.

Trains often run through the night, so you may have to get off at stations very early in the morning. On some services the booking of a sleeper ticket is compulsory. The *Thomas Cook European Timetable* (*see p188*) contains schedules for all international rail services. *www.raileurope.co.uk www.trainseurope.co.uk www.seat61.com*

By road

There are land crossings into Bulgaria through Romania, Greece, Turkey and Serbia. Travelling through Greece is the easiest and shortest option from the UK, with a well-organised and comfortable Italy–Greece ferry service (try **Superfast Ferries**: *www.superfast.com*) allowing you to reach Bulgaria from the UK in four days. Sail from Ancona or Bari in Italy to Iguoumenitsa or Patras on the west coast of Greece for onward road travel to the land border at Kulata, south of Sofia in Bulgaria.

Make sure you have insurance cover for the vehicle – this may involve getting a Green Card extension to your normal insurance policy.

By coach

Eurolines (*www.eurolines.co.uk*) runs several services per week from locations in the UK to Bulgaria, though this may involve transfers. The journey takes at least three days.

Camping

Facilities for campers are poor compared with Western European countries. Many have had little investment since the communist era. The best sites are on the Black Sea coast, although these get crowded in July and August, when it's best to book in advance, and they close in winter (Oct–May).

Children

Stocks of essentials such as nappies and baby food can be found in towns all across Bulgaria but you may have problems finding child-friendly changing places. High seats in restaurants are non-existent outside the major package-tour hotels.

If you travel with children during the summer, make sure you protect them adequately against the strong sun. Mosquitoes may be a problem, so take insect repellent, and after country walks check for midge or tick bites. Don't allow children to play with animals, as rabies, although not common, is a danger.

Climate

Bulgarian weather is characterised by hot dry summers and cool-to-cold, damp winters (*see pp6–8*).

Summer temperatures are tempered in the east by the Black Sea. The mountains receive more rain and snow

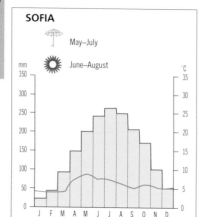

SOFIA

May–July

June–August

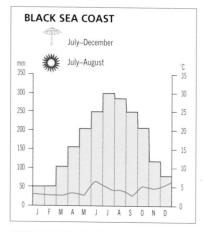

BLACK SEA COAST

July–December

July–August

WEATHER CONVERSION CHART

25.4mm = 1 inch

°F = 1.8 × °C + 32

than the plains, but winter can produce massive rain and snowfall across the whole country.

Crime

You'll be at a relatively low risk of becoming a victim of serious crime in Bulgaria. However, so-called petty crime such as theft (especially from vehicles) can be a problem in big cities or on the Black Sea coast. Take the following precautions to minimise your chances of a loss:

• Do not leave valuables in a car and leave nothing on show.
• Don't carry large amounts of cash or valuables with you.
• Deposit valuables in the hotel safe.
• Take extra care at ATMs.
• Carry handbags over your shoulder and across your chest to discourage bag snatchers.
• Don't leave valuables unattended on the beach or in cafés and restaurants.

Customs regulations

Non-EU travellers over 16 are allowed to take in the following items duty-free:
200 cigarettes or 250g (8³⁄₄oz) of tobacco; 2 litres (3¹⁄₂pt) of wine or 1 litre (1³⁄₄pt) of stronger alcohol; 250ml (8³⁄₄oz) of perfume.

Driving

Bulgaria drives on the right, overtaking on the left. Roads vary greatly in quality. The main link roads are acceptable but may have areas where the upper layer of tarmac has been removed. Minor roads are in poor condition and riddled with potholes.

Road signs are in Cyrillic only (except in Sofia and on the Black Sea coast), and some are missing, making navigation a challenge.

Speed limits for cars are 120kph (75mph) on dual carriageways, 90kph (56mph) on main roads and 50kph (31mph) in urban areas. Seat belts are compulsory for drivers and front-seat passengers, and helmets are compulsory for motorcyclists. The blood-alcohol limit is 0.05 per cent and it is strictly enforced. It's compulsory to wait with the vehicle until the police arrive if you have an accident. Fines for infractions are high and your licence could be suspended for three months.

CONVERSION TABLE

FROM	TO	MULTIPLY BY
Inches	Centimetres	2.54
Feet	Metres	0.3048
Yards	Metres	0.9144
Miles	Kilometres	1.6090
Acres	Hectares	0.4047
Gallons	Litres	4.5460
Ounces	Grams	28.35
Pounds	Grams	453.6
Pounds	Kilograms	0.4536
Tons	Tonnes	1.0160

To convert back, for example from centimetres to inches, divide by the number in the third column.

Car rental

Cars can be rented in Sofia and in the major resorts and towns. The international car-rental companies may charge up to 50 per cent more than a local agency; you will, however, get a new car and good backup if you have a problem. Renting through a local agency will be cheaper but cars may be older and not all companies accept credit cards, which means leaving cash as a deposit (normally around €150). Many Bulgarian travel agencies/commercial tourist offices will also organise car rental.

Driving licences

Your domestic driving licence is recognised in Bulgaria as long as you stay less than three months. You will need to have had a full licence for at least one year and be over 21 to rent a vehicle.

Electricity

Bulgaria uses 220V AC for its supply. Plugs are the two-pinned variety, so travellers from the UK will need an adaptor.

Embassies and consulates

All foreign embassies and consulates are located in the capital, Sofia. See *www.embassyworld.com*

UK
ul. Moskovska 9. Tel: (02) 933 9222; fax: (02) 933 9250.

USA
ul. Koziak 16. Tel: (02) 953 5100; fax: (02) 937 5320.

Australian consulate
ul. Trakia 37. Tel: (02) 946 1334; fax: (02) 946 1704.

Canadian consulate
ul. Pozitano 7. Tel: (02) 969 9710.

Republic of Ireland
ul. Bacho Kiro 26. Tel: (02) 985 3425.

Emergency telephone numbers

Fire *160*

Ambulance *150*

Police *166*

The EU-wide emergency number *112* has been implemented in Bulgaria, although with some teething problems.

Health

There are no compulsory inoculations for travel to Bulgaria.

There is basic healthcare (a clinic) in most small towns and there are hospitals in major towns, but these are under-equipped by Western European standards. Sofia has the best-equipped and also has several private hospitals. Doctors are well trained and most speak some English. *See Insurance below.*

Pharmacies sell many drugs over the counter; however, brand names vary, so if you need a specific medication/drug take an empty packet with you to aid the pharmacist.

Several minor nuisances should be watched for. Mosquitoes can be a problem so carry repellent and cover arms and legs in the evenings. It is wise to cover legs and arms when hiking.

Websites for health and travel advice from the British government: *www.doh.gov.uk, www.fco.gov.uk* Websites for American travellers: *www.cdc.gov/travel* and *www.healthfinder.com* Useful tips and information: *www.travelhealth.co.uk* World Health Organization: *www.who.int/en*

Insurance

It is highly recommended that you arrange travel insurance before travelling to Bulgaria. Bulgaria's entry to the EU has led to some reciprocal health schemes with other EU countries such as Britain, but as yet this is not widespread, and travel insurance is advisable for all travellers. You will need to make a police report for non-medical claims and ensure you keep any receipts for medical treatment. Consider keeping a copy of your policy and emergency contact numbers in your email account.

Lost property

Airports and railway stations have lost property departments, otherwise try the local police station. You'll need an official police report to make an insurance claim for any lost property. If you lose your passport, contact your embassy or consulate.

Maps

You can buy maps of Bulgaria at all major bookshops, but these may be in Cyrillic only. **Domino** (*www.domino.bg*) produces the best range.

Media

The *Sofia Echo* (*www.sofiaecho.com*) is an English-language newspaper published each Friday. It has details of entertainment listings as well as news. Foreign newspapers are available in Sofia and the Black Sea resorts, although these may be one day old. Internet cafés are common and access is cheap.

Money matters
Credit cards
Credit cards are not universally accepted across Bulgaria but their use is gaining ground. If you intend to stay in the capital or on the Black Sea you'll find their use more widespread (though you may be subject to a surcharge), but it's still better to ask at hotels, restaurants and petrol stations before you order if you intend to pay with a card (some have window stickers but no card facilities!). It is also wise to carry enough cash to cover your daily needs just in case. You can use your credit card to get cash advances over the counter in some banks.

Currency
Bulgarian currency is the lev, leva in the plural, abbreviated lv in shops, hotels and restaurants, or BGN in banks and bureaux de change. One lev is made up of 100 stotinki, with note denominations of 2, 5, 10, 20, 50 and 100 leva and coins of 1, 2, 5, 10, 20 and 50 stotinki, and 1 lev. The euro is sometimes accepted because the lev is pegged to the European currency. All other currencies fluctuate with the exchange markets. If bringing foreign banknotes to exchange in Bulgaria, ensure that none are defaced or torn as they may be refused.

Foreign exchange
Although prices for restaurants and budget hotels will be quoted in leva, most expensive purchases (higher-grade hotels, car hire, excursions, etc) will be quoted in euros. It will be possible to pay for these items in most forms of foreign currency at the day's exchange rate. Foreign currency can be exchanged at bureaux de change, which are plentiful at resorts and in major towns. Most large banks will also offer an exchange-rate facility. Travellers will find it easier if they carry US dollars, euros or pounds sterling rather than any other foreign currency, which may be less easy to change.

Traveller's cheques are not as easy to cash as foreign currency (though they are more secure than cash, as you can get them replaced if they are lost or stolen).

ATMs are becoming more numerous and you will certainly be able to get cash in Sofia and the Black Sea coast resorts.

Opening hours
Normal business hours are Mon–Fri 9am–5pm. Government offices will close for an hour at lunchtime (any time between noon and 2pm) but commercial organisations generally don't. Shops open Mon–Fri 9am–7pm and Sat 9am–1pm, but have extended hours in summer, especially in Sofia and on the Black Sea coast. Post offices are open Mon–Fri 8am–6pm. Banks are open Mon–Fri 9am–4pm. Museums are generally open 10am–5.30pm but are closed at least one day and many close at lunchtimes for one hour. Opening times change frequently.

(*Cont. on p186*)

Language

Bulgarian is a Slavic language written in Cyrillic script, an alphabet with
30 letters. Though most workers in the tourist industry speak some English, it
will certainly help your visit if you have a basic understanding of this alphabet.

THE CYRILLIC ALPHABET

All letters are pronounced as their Roman equivalents in English unless
indicated otherwise.

Capital	Lower-case	Roman	Pronunciation
А	а	a	short as in 'fat'
Б	б	b	
В	в	v	
Г	г	g	hard as in 'go'
Д	д	d	
Е	е	e	
Ж	ж	zh	as the s in 'treasure'
З	з	z	
И	и	i	
Й	й	y	
К	к	k	
Л	л	l	
М	м	m	
Н	н	n	
О	о	o	short as in 'hot'
П	п	p	
Р	р	r	a rolling r like that of French
С	с	s	
Т	т	t	
У	у	oo	as in 'shoot'
Ф	ф	f	
Х	х	ch	like the ch of Scottish 'loch'
Ц	ц	ts	as in the word 'bets'
Ч	ч	ch	as in 'chop'
Ш	ш	sh	as in 'shop'
Щ	щ	sht	as the '-shed' in 'rushed' but shorter
Ъ	ъ	u	short u sound like German 'ö' or French 'eu'
Ь	ь		no phonetic value
Я	я	ya	a short hard sound
Ю	ю	yu	a short hard sound

PHRASES

Here are a few helpful phrases written in Cyrillic script, then in Roman script so
that you can understand how to pronounce them.

English	Cyrillic	Pronunciation
Hello	Здравейте	zdraveyte
Goodbye	Довиждане	dovizhdane
Yes	Да	da
No	Не	ne
Please	Моля	molya
Thank you	Благодаря	blagodarya
Do you speak English?	Говорите ли английски?	govorite li angliyski?
I don't understand	Аз не разбирам	az ne razbiram
I am looking for the/a	Търся	tursya
Bank	Банка	banka
Museum	Музея	moozeya
Post office	Поща	poshta
Toilet	Тоалетна	toaletna
Tourist office	Бюрото за туризъм	byuroto za toorizum
Hotel	Хотел	khotel
How much is it?	Колко струва?	kolko stroova?
Monday	Понеделник	ponedelnik
Tuesday	Вторник	vtornik
Wednesday	Сряда	sryada
Thursday	Четвъртък	chetvurtuk
Friday	Петък	petuk
Saturday	Събота	subota
Sunday	Неделя	nedelya
One	Едно	edno
Two	Две	dve
Three	Три	tri
Four	Четири	chetiri
Five	Пет	pet
Six	Шест	shest
Seven	Седем	sedem
Eight	Осем	osem
Nine	Девет	devet
Ten	Десет	deset
One hundred	Сто	sto
Help!	Помош!	pomosh!

Police

Police officers wear navy blue uniforms, rather like overalls. They aren't universally helpful and many don't speak English, but they are not usually a problem for ordinary law-abiding visitors (although some elicit bribes from motorists over minor infractions). There are also numerous armed private security guards in shops and banks; they have no jurisdiction under law but have been employed to thwart shoplifters and criminal gangs. If this makes Bulgaria sound like a dangerous or lawless place, don't worry, because it isn't.

Emergency tel: 166.

Post offices

Post office signs are yellow with a black bugle imprinted on them. You'll find post offices in all major towns, and many postboxes, also yellow. Postcard shops in the resorts will sell stamps.

Public holidays

The following dates are official holidays in Bulgaria. All government buildings and banks will be closed, but not commercial businesses. Public transport also operates normally.

1 Jan New Year's Day
3 Mar Liberation or National Day
Mar/Apr Good Friday and Easter Sunday
1 May Labour Day
24 May Bulgarian Culture Day
6 Sept National Day or Unification Day
22 Sept Bulgarian Independence Day
25–26 Dec Christmas

A more traditional means of transport

Stamp your ticket when you board a tram, or risk a fine

Public transport

Air

Internal flights are limited to travel between Sofia and Varna and Burgas airports on the Black Sea coast. Flights run throughout the year, with more in summer. There are other airlines running summer flights (normally Apr–Oct), with prices much the same as, or sometimes cheaper than, the main carrier.

Buses

A network of public buses run by the government connects almost all towns and villages in the country. Fares are cheap but many buses are antiquated and you can't book ahead. In larger

towns and cities modern private bus services now offer a much more acceptable alternative and a reliable way to get around, with the added advantage that you can book tickets in advance from the ticket office at the bus station.

Minibuses link the resorts along the Black Sea coast. You can normally buy tickets from the driver.

Taxis

Taxis are painted yellow and are numerous in cities and resorts. They can be flagged down in the street. They must by law have a working meter but can be chartered for longer trips – negotiate with the driver. Taxi drivers along the Black Sea coast and around the railway station and airport in Sofia have a reputation for overcharging, so don't agree to a flat rate or believe stories of meters not working.

Trains
Bulgarski Durzhavni Zheleznitsi (*www.bdz.bg*), the Bulgarian state railway, has a comprehensive network linking all the major settlements. It is cheap, but the rolling stock and track are not up to Western standards. Trains are classified as *ekspresen* (express), *burz* (fast) and *putnicheski* (slow). First-class fares are only around 20 per cent higher than second class. Bookable sleeper couchettes are available on longer journeys.

Advance tickets are recommended if you want to travel to the Black Sea from Sofia. Most European rail passes are valid in Bulgaria, and the Bulgarian system is also linked to the Euro-Domino pass. Timetables are available but are only in Cyrillic. For a timetable of the main Bulgarian rail services, consult the *Thomas Cook European Timetable*, published monthly and available from UK branches of Thomas Cook or through *tel: 01733 416477 (UK), 1800 322 3834 (US); www.thomascookpublishing.com*

Sustainable tourism
Thomas Cook is a strong advocate of ethical and fairly traded tourism and believes that the travel experience

should be as good for the places visited as it is for the people who visit them. That's why we firmly support The Travel Foundation, a charity that develops solutions to help improve and protect holiday destinations, their environment, traditions and culture. To find out what you can do to make a positive difference to the places you travel to and the people who live there, please visit *www.makeholidaysgreener.org.uk*

Telephones
Your mobile phone should work throughout Bulgaria – except in some remote areas – and for most travellers this usually suffices. The public telephone system is undergoing rapid development, with booths in major cities and towns offering international direct dialling by credit card (where the instructions will be shown in English) or local phonecard.

Bulgarian Telecommunications Company (БТС) is the national provider and it has a network of call centres in all major towns. Here you can make calls, including long-distance and international calls, and pay for them on completion.

Modern hotels will usually have a direct-dial phone system, but they often add extortionate surcharges for calls. Ask about charges before you make the decision to ring home.

The country code for phoning from abroad to Bulgaria is *359*; then omit the first *0* in the Bulgarian area code that

follows. To make an international call from inside Bulgaria, dial *00* followed by the country code, for example:
USA and Canada *00 1*
UK *00 44*
Ireland *00 353*
Australia *00 61*
New Zealand *00 64*

Time

Bulgaria is on Eastern European time, two hours ahead of the UK. It is ten hours ahead of the US West Coast and seven ahead of the East Coast, nine hours behind New Zealand, five behind West Coast Australia and seven behind East Coast Australia. Clocks change on the last Sundays in March and October.

Tipping

Some hotels and restaurants add a service charge to the bill. If not, a 10 per cent tip is usual if the service has been good. Don't put tips in the hand, as this is socially unacceptable. Taxi drivers may round the fare up, in which case they don't need a tip.

Toilets

Most toilets are the sit-on variety, though you may find some 'hole in the floor' types in the southeast. Public toilets are generally poor in quality and cleanliness, even though there is usually a charge to use them. It is better to try to use facilities in museums (generally good) or bar/restaurants (of mixed quality). Always carry a supply of toilet paper with you.

Tourist information

Bulgaria is still a very long way from providing a comprehensive and integrated tourist information service. Most 'tourist offices' in towns are commercial organisations geared to booking accommodation and bus tours.

Before you travel you can obtain general brochures from your local Bulgarian National Tourist Office or Embassy at one of these addresses:
Australia *33 Culgoa Cct, O'Malley, Canberra ACT. Tel: (02) 6286 9700.*
Canada *325 Stewart Street, Ottawa, Ontario K1N 6K5. Tel: 0613 789 3215.*
UK *186–188 Queen's Gate, London SW7 5HL. Tel: 020 7584 9400.*
USA *1621 22nd St NW, Washington DC 20008. Tel: 0202 387 0174.*

Websites

Bulgaria State Agency for Tourism website, *www.bulgariatravel.org* General tourist site for Bulgaria, *www.bulgarian-tourism.com* Information on rural tourism, *www.ruralbulgaria.com*

Travellers with disabilities

Provision for travellers with mobility problems is poor. Always make specific enquiries with hotels if you require specially equipped rooms.

A guide to international airlines that have facilities for passengers with disabilities can be found at *www.allgohere.com*

Index

Acknowledgements

Thomas Cook Publishing wishes to thank PETE BENNETT, to whom the copyright belongs, for the photographs in this book, except for the following images:
DREAMSTIME 1 (IOSHERTZ), 51 (IANKO), 84 (SHOWTURTLE), 119 (KATARINA21), 138 (JORDAN RUSEV)
FOTOLIA 99 (ANTON GAVRAILOV), 100 (YAVOR NIKOLOV), 106 (PATRICIA FARRELL)
ROSS HILTON 88, 91, 136, 160, 186
IMAGES FROM BULGARIA/KIRIL KAPUSTIN 169
STOCKAPHOTO 111, 163
VASILE SZAKACS 21, 32, 33, 45, 68, 122, 164
WIKIMEDIA COMMONS 28 (PODOBOQ@FLICKR), 67 (NANKO LAZAROV), 80 (NIKOLA GRUEV),
127 (ZIODAVE/FLICKR), 139 (MILEN LASKOV), 187 (IVAN IVANOV)
WORLD PICTURES/PHOTOSHOT 29, 43, 56, 85, 112, 118, 123, 129, 145
THOMAS COOK 30, 157

For CAMBRIDGE PUBLISHING MANAGEMENT LIMITED
Project editor: Ed Robinson
Typesetter: Paul Queripel
Proofreaders: Penny Isaac & Jan McCann
Indexer: Marie Lorimer

SEND YOUR THOUGHTS TO
BOOKS@THOMASCOOK.COM

We're committed to providing the very best up-to-date information in our travel guides and constantly strive to make them as useful as they can be. You can help us to improve future editions by letting us have your feedback. If you've made a wonderful discovery on your travels that we don't already feature, if you'd like to inform us about recent changes to anything that we do include, or if you simply want to let us know your thoughts about this guidebook and how we can make it even better – we'd love to hear from you.

Send us ideas, discoveries and recommendations today and then look out for your valuable input in the next edition of this title.

Emails to the above address, or letters to the traveller guides Series Editor, Thomas Cook Publishing, PO Box 227, Coningsby Road, Peterborough PE3 8SB, UK.

Please don't forget to let us know which title your feedback refers to!